The Man
Who Wanted The World

By the Same Author

    THOMAS COKE—a play (M.M.S.)
    THE PERILOUS ADVENTURE (with Bill Ream) (M.M.S.)

Published in India

    A HANDBOOK TO THE NORTH-WEST FRONTIER
    A BOOK ABOUT INDIA
    FEASTS AND FESTIVALS OF INDIA

Thomas Coke

The Man
Who Wanted the World

THE STORY OF THOMAS COKE

by
Cyril J. Davey

METHODIST MISSIONARY SOCIETY
(CARGATE PRESS)
25 Marylebone Road, London, N.W.1
1947

Made and Printed in Great Britain by
Hazell, Watson & Viney Ltd., London and Aylesbury

TO

MY MOTHER

AND IN MEMORY OF

MY FATHER

CONTENTS

SOME IMPORTANT DATES

1747 Born at Brecon

1764 Matriculated at Oxford

1770 Curate at Petherton

1772 Conversion

1776 Expelled from South Petherton
Joins the Methodists

1782 First Visit to Ireland

1783 The Deed of Declaration

1784 The Plan for Missions

1784 Ordination by John Wesley
First Visit to America

1786 Lands in the West Indies

1787 Second Visit to America

1788 Second Visit to West Indies
Third Visit to America

1789 The First Missionary Committee Formed

1790 Fourth Visit to America
Third Visit to West Indies

1791 John Wesley's Death

1792 Visits France
Fifth Visit to America
Fourth Visit to West Indies
Gains Toleration for West Indian Methodist
Slaves

1794 Visits Holland

1795 Sierra Leone Project Fails

1796 Sixth Visit to America
Joins American Conference

1797 Seventh Visit to America
Elected President of British Conference

INTRODUCTION

The life of Dr. Thomas Coke is one of the great epics of the Christian Church, and it is a serious loss that it is so little known. He travelled more miles on his voyages than almost any man of his time, save professional sailors, and few men since the days of St. Paul could more aptly have taken the Apostle's words to themselves—"in journeyings often, in perils of waters, in perils of robbers, in perils by my own countrymen . . . in perils in the wilderness, in perils in the sea . . . in labour and travail, in watchings often, in hunger and thirst, in fastings often, in cold and nakedness. Beside those things that are without, there is that which presseth upon me daily, anxiety for all the churches."

Here and there in the West Indies there is a church —perhaps the second or third on the same site, that bears Coke's name and immortalises his memory. But his true memorial is in the living Church that exists through those far-stretching islands and elsewhere, and in the missionary work of the Methodist Church which he founded and to which he devoted his life.

This book is the story of that life. It has been produced in connection with the bi-centenary of Coke's birth on September 9th, 1747. At the time of his death Mr. F. Deaville Walker was engaged on a full-length biography of Coke for which he had collected material for many years, but only the first few chapters were completed. It may be finished by another hand, but, in the meantime, here is Mr. Davey's book, shorter, but con-

taining the essential facts set forth in the most attractive
fashion.

I have been asked to write an introduction to it, perhaps because I had the pleasure of reading it in serial
form as it was written, and came to look forward to the
successive instalments with some impatience. I have no
doubt that it will move others in the same way, and will
inspire them so to live and serve that they will follow
Coke's example and find it—

> "Life's best joy to see Thy praise
> Fly on wings of gospel light."

It is that quality of inspiration which the Church needs
to-day.

W. J. NOBLE.

THE WORLD HE WANTED

THOMAS COKE was born eight years before Clive won the Battle of Plassey and broke the power of France in India. He died a few months before the battle of Waterloo, at the age of sixty-six. For almost forty years, during that time, Britain was at war, and during the last twenty years of his life Napoleon was the master of Europe and had his armies in almost every country except Britain. Out of eighteen voyages across the Atlantic, ten were undertaken with the knowledge that the French had their fleets at sea and appeared to be the masters of it.

When he was born peace had been made, temporarily, between Britain and her enemies, France and Spain, after the nine years of war known as the Wars of Jenkins' Ear and the Austrian Succession. England had been threatened within by the Rebellion of Prince Charlie, the Young Pretender, in 1745. He was only six years old when France and Britain took up the struggle again at sea, in Canada and in India.

Before he went to Oxford, at the age of sixteen, France had been decisively worsted in the West Indies, in India and in America. Dupleix had fought a series of losing actions and, largely due to the generalship of the East India Company's clerk, Robert Clive, Britain came out of the war with almost full control of India and Indian trading rights. Wolfe had been killed on the Plains of Abraham above Quebec, but not before he knew that the French General, Montcalm, had lost the day and, in doing so, had lost Canada to the British. In the West Indies, Rodney had regained most of the islands which had been conquered by France in the early stages of the war.

These gains to the growing empire in the east and west were offset by the inevitable breaking away of the old American Colonies. Alienated by an irresponsible and unimaginative Government in England, the colonists followed a series of ineffective protests against abuses by declaring war in 1773, just after Coke had gone to his first curacy. In the year that he finally joined the Methodists, 1776, America published her Declaration of Independence, and though the war dragged on for another seven years there could be no doubt of the issue.

While Coke was paying his second visit to the West Indies, in 1788, the French Revolution began. Though many in England, the romantic poets amongst them, welcomed the rebellion of the peasantry against the tyranny of the French aristocrats, they were soon disillusioned by the Reign of Terror, and five years after the Revolution began, France under Napoleon, and Britain under the premiership of William Pitt, were at war once more. The struggle went on until after Coke's death, and during most of the time, in spite of Nelson's brilliant seamanship and Wellington's determined but abortive assaults on the Iberian Peninsula, Britain was on the edge of defeat.

The war had not touched Africa closely, though British interests had increased there through the ceding of Cape Colony by the Dutch in 1793, and the gaining of Sierra Leone from native chiefs two years earlier.

Three hundred years had passed since the Spaniards

first raised the standards of Ferdinand and Isabella on the shores of the New World. The coasts of Africa had been known to navigators and the way to the East opened up for about the same period. China was still a closed country to foreigners, though the East Indies had been colonised by the Dutch. Ceylon became a Crown Colony in 1793. The Pacific alone remained unexplored when Coke was born. One of the books he notes down with great interest as having been read on his first voyage to America, however, is Captain Cook's *Voyages*. Cook, between 1768 and 1775, had paid two visits of reconnaissance to the Southern Pacific. On the first he had circumnavigated New Zealand and made a landfall in Eastern Australia, and on the second he had discovered a number of the larger island groups of the South Seas. Britain declared Australia a Colony when the first party of transported convicts was settled in Botany Bay in 1788.

Such was the world Coke knew. It was a world of imperial expansion, with Canada, India, Ceylon, parts of Africa and finally Australasia coming under British rule. It was a world of war, in which travel was dangerous by land or sea, in Europe or the Atlantic. It was also very much a world in which governments thought mainly of expansion or defence and were, in the main, utterly indifferent to the interests of religion. Christianity had become a western faith and, both in Roman Catholic and Protestant lands, a largely ineffective one.

In Britain the Established Church had, until the middle of the century, been almost entirely moribund. Even the influence of the "religious societies" which began in Queen Anne's reign had died away. In France, as in Spain and other Catholic countries, the Church was associated in the popular mind with the oppressive aristocracy. In large parts of Wales, Scotland and Ireland an illiterate population knew nothing of the Bible or the gospel. America, founded in a passion for political and religious freedom, maintained much of the old puritanism on the east coast, where religious life was leavened by Continental immigrants from Holland and Germany, but in the pioneer districts farther south and west there were practically no ministrations from the Established Church, which was controlled by the Bishop of London from a land thousands of miles away.

In British Colonies Anglican clergymen and chaplains officiated with a general degree of casualness. Undoubtedly there were sincere men in the West Indies, in the service of the East India Company and in the Army, but neither their training nor the circumstances in which they lived tended to increase or even maintain any kind of religious zeal. In any case, their ministry was intended only for British people.

The negro slaves of America and the West Indies, the Africans of the West Coast and the Cape, the Tamils and Ceylonese of Ceylon, the Hindus in India and the aboriginal people and cannibals of Australia and the South Sea Islands were by most people regarded as inferior beings who could not be expected either to respond to or even to need the Christian gospel. "Leave them alone," was the order of officialdom. "When God chooses to convert the heathen He will do so without our aid—though we doubt if He wishes to convert them at all," was the attitude of the Church.

Into this situation at home came the Evangelical Revival and Methodism, bringing a new surging life to every part of Britain's agricultural and new industrial areas, and into America. Religion came to be a force in the life of the people, and from it sprang movements of regeneration and reform which, in the hundred years that followed, touched every part of the national life.

Into this world situation was born Thomas Coke, a Welshman who wanted the world for Christ.

CHAPTER ONE

THE BEGINNING
(1747–1776)

THE old man, who had so often walked this road to the court-house, stepped more proudly one summer morning in 1770 than he had done since he was first appointed a bailiff of Brecon more than thirty years earlier. Everywhere his equals saluted him with respect, while the lesser folk of the town touched their forelocks with more courtesy than they showed to many of their masters. Bartholomew Coke returned their salutes without realising that he did so. He noticed the loveliness of the Vale of Usk, in which Brecon was set, as little as he did the dilapidation of many of its houses. Neither the familiar ruins of the old castle nor the remains of the Benedictine Priory, once a cell of Battle Abbey far away on the south coast, held his attention. He saw only the young man at his side.

Bartholomew had known many tragedies and more happiness in his long life. His position had always been assured, as the son of a local rector, and when he set up in Brecon as an apothecary both his skill and his kindness won him so many patients and friends that few of the local folk ever troubled to go to a physician. He had held the offices of bailiff, alderman and justice of the peace for many years in the borough. He and Anne, his wife, had known sadness, too, when their first two sons died in infancy and they had thought there would never be another child in their home.

Then, in 1747, Thomas had been born.

And now, twenty-three years later, young Thomas—still hardly more than a boy, it seemed, though he had been to Oxford and become a bachelor of arts—was going with him to the court-house in the proudest moment of his life. Thomas Coke was, that day, to be sworn in as a justice of the peace and chief magistrate of the borough. What an honour for so young a man! And yet, as he watched him taking the oath a little later, the old man was not surprised.

Thomas was short and stocky; later he would put on a good deal of weight, though that would never make him a figure of fun. His bearing was good; it was that of the born aristocrat, and would win him his way into many homes and hearts amongst the nobility. His round face, with its ruddy complexion, was now serious, but even in this mood there was a sense of urgency and eagerness about him that was typical of the man. His impatience to be about the matter in his heart, his passion to see results, might lead him into false positions, impair his judgment, lead to accusations of hastiness and excessive zeal which would not be unfounded —but these were the qualities which, nevertheless, had brought him so quickly into prominence and would always make him a leader amongst men.

"He will not stay here," thought old Bartholomew. "This is too small a place. He may become anything he wishes. A bishop, an archbishop perhaps, even the Lord Chancellor of England." His mind wandered back to the days when young Thomas had been a schoolboy in Brecon, at the college which Henry VII founded "for the encouragement of preaching and teaching, and good literature and the dedication of youth," and then he thought of how he had seen him off to Oxford, a youth of sixteen, and of how there, at Jesus College, he had met men who were to be great in their time, men with whom Thomas might climb to success.

It was perhaps good for his peace of mind that Bartholomew had not seen all that his son did at Oxford. The reports that came in the boy's letters were full of exciting things. He told something of Jesus College and its history since it had been founded by their own fellow-townsman, Dr. Hugh Price. He wrote of his life as a "gentleman commoner." He exulted in his matriculation and his degree of bachelor. He mentioned names —Jenkinson, Addington, Smith—of men who were to be famous, and with whom he was to have dealings later, as the Lords Liverpool, Addington and Eldon, the Lord Chancellor.

His father knew less about Oxford than Robert Southey, the Laureate, who later wrote a life of John Wesley which men still read, and who vowed, "I never shall send a child of mine to . . . a University. I may not be able to instruct him so well in logic or languages, but at least I can preserve him from vice."

What Thomas did not admit to his father was the way he allowed his tutor and his fellow-students to persuade him into the more fashionable, if less degraded, vices of the University. He developed a fondness for dancing. He frequented the disreputable theatres, with their salacious Restoration plays. He was to be found at the gaming-tables where, if he did not sit through the night and day like the noble Lord Sandwich, who refused to go away even for his meals, he managed to squander a good deal of money and waste a great deal of time.

More serious than this outward dissipation, however, was the effect on his mind of the current scepticism represented by his tutor. Voltaire, Rousseau and Lessing were the moulders of progressive thought, and Thomas followed them in his deistical, agnostic attitude to religious things.

There was too much of the mystical Welshman in him to allow him to be a slave to such materialism for long. A word from a friend here, the reading of a serious book by Bishop Sherlock there, made him long to be free of his way of living. A phrase in Alleine's *Alarm to the Unconverted*—the very title was enough to call him to a halt—stuck in his mind. "There is a murderer in your bosom." Coke knew what that meant. His best self killed, his dreams unrealised.

When he returned to Brecon he was a changed man. He was anxious to be of service, and his mind was already turning over the problem of whether he could not best serve the day—and still find advancement and success—within the Church.

His father was too wise to turn him aside and persuade him to remain in Brecon, but, like Thomas himself, he looked about for a wide door into the Church rather than see his son enter it through some curacy, unheeded and unacknowledged.

Whether or not it had always been in his mind to enter the Church we do not know, and certainly he had grave doubts about his fitness for ordination. In addition, the lure of Brecon, with its assured position there in society and congenial work, must at times have been very strong. The more he thought of it, however, the less he was able to escape the conviction that he must take orders, and, the same year in which he was appointed chief magistrate of the borough, he made the decision which was to drive him out for ever from a life of security and ease into one of turmoil, adventure and unending labour.

There were three ways of entering the Church. The first was the purchase of a benefice which would remain his own. Neither he nor his father had sufficient money for such a venture, it seems, and the second way had many attractions. This was to secure the patronage of some great man who would put him into a living which he controlled. As a rule, such patrons did not inquire too closely into the lives of their protégés and, provided the clergyman was able to entertain his patron when he came to stay, to share the pleasures of the town or the pursuits of the country, and to play whist and drink measure for measure with the local gentry and squires, his life would not be greatly disturbed and, indeed, he might rapidly gain such promotion that he could afford to employ his own curate and, himself, go and live where he would and do what he liked. Absentee clergy were a curse of the countryside. Such a genial patron Coke seemed to have found. He had assisted a certain gentleman of consequence to secure his seat in a local election to Parliament, and had every reason to hope that he would be rewarded suitably with a prebend's stall in Worcester Cathedral. It would indeed have been a broad door into the Church, through which many would see him enter.

Patronage is fickle in its favours and absent-minded about its promises. The local gentleman forgot his electioneering helper, and Coke had to seek the third entrance into his chosen career. It was the humble way of becoming a curate in an unsought parish, the assistant of a parson with little love for his work. Coke was disappointed about his failure to enter the cathedral, and had no great liking for the Somersetshire village of South Petherton to which he went, though the gentry were friendly enough and made up for some of his acquaintances at home. Their houses were open to him, and he passed pleasant evenings with them over the whist table. The villagers, on the other hand, were rough, crude and hard to understand. Their amusements were simple and centred round the taprooms and the cockpits of the local inns. Those who did not share these interests were, to Coke's mind, harsh, fanatical and over-pious—the followers of a dissenting minister whom the vicar and his curate disliked and despised.

The young curate could not be held long by the pleasures of South Petherton's society, any more than he was for long under the influence of his more ribald and vicious friends at Oxford. He had given up a life of security and ease in Brecon because he felt called to the Church, and the fact that he hoped for some of its higher offices was nothing to his discredit. He knew without any doubt that he was born to exercise authority, but the love he had for the Church was deep and sincere. No moving religious experience had shaken him, it is true—though his volatile Welsh temperament might not resist it when it came—and his churchman-ship was of the cold, "high" type of the early Wesleys. The Bishops of Exeter, and Bath and Wells, already had their eye on him as a likely man for preferment, and when, in 1775, he became a doctor of civil law, it seemed certain that he would rise high and rapidly in the Church he loved.

At the very time the authorities of the Church were thinking of promotion, his parishioners were growing hostile and beginning to wonder how they could get rid of him.

The trouble with him, in their view, was that he had become a "fanatic."

The process began in Oxford, when he turned from

scepticism to the Church. It was continued in Brecon, when he resolved to devote himself to the Church. It went on in South Petherton, when he found himself interested, in spite of his better judgment, in the dissenting minister, Hull, and his success in changing drunken, loutish villagers into decent men and women. At this time he was sufficiently rigid in his churchmanship to refuse to allow the dissenter to enter his own house, or to agree to meet him where he was invited. A meeting was eventually arranged, though without any apparent friendship arising from it.

Then, a couple of years after his arrival in the village, a visitor came to stay. He was Thomas Maxfield, and Coke knew him for one of the earliest helpers of that notorious emotionalist, who had broken so many of the traditions of the Church, John Wesley. Maxfield had been ordained by the Bishop of Londonderry specifically, in his own episcopal phrase, "to assist that good man, John Wesley, in order that he may not work himself to death." Coke had no liking for the Wesleys or their ways, but he discovered a tremendous respect for Maxfield. To his surprise he found that the clergyman had an even greater power over men than the local dissenting minister, and that he was content to be a friend of a poor, unknown man who was a class-leader amongst the local Methodists.

Up to this time Coke had been greatly popular with the people of South Petherton. He was always a man of easy friendliness and his preaching was simple but sincere. Much of his time was given to the ordinary people, and his visits to the great houses grew less and less frequent. The result was that the church was thronged with villagers. There was not room for those who wanted to worship. Coke went to his more noble

South Petherton Church. House in which Coke lodged to right.

acquaintances and begged for money to build a gallery in the church.

The answer was brief, but simple. "Since you have not enough interest in us even to play whist with us, Mr. Coke, you may go elsewhere for your money. If you desire a churchful of village ruffians, they—or you— may pay for their accommodation."

The village folk could not afford to build a gallery— the curate could, with some self-sacrifice, and did so, with his own money.

Coke watched and listened as Maxfield dealt with these men and women who thronged his own church, and was amazed at the results. His suspicions of the followers and associates of the Wesleys began to dissolve, and, with Maxfield, he talked far into the night and through long days about the truths they preached, the methods they used and the experience they shared. Here was a man and a message which spoke clearly to his own heart and stirred him, as a Welshman can be stirred, to the depths of his being.

Maxfield went away. Coke stayed, and thought much. Then, one day, something happened.

He was walking through the country lanes, on his way to preach in a neighbouring village. As he went he pondered what he was going to say. Suddenly, in his own words, "I was given a vivid consciousness of the divine presence, and from this moment became a new creature."

His conversion was as simple—to outsiders, as abrupt —as that.

The year was 1772. He had been just two years a curate.

The results of this new experience were, to his congregation, surprising, and, to many of those who, like a famous dean of Exeter, were "stern foes to enthusiasm in religion," shocking in the extreme. The news spread swiftly of what was happening.

"The parson has been converted!"

"He no longer reads his sermons from a book . . ."

". . . and, what is worse, he prays without using the prayer-book."

"The curate makes them sing hymns—*songs!*—in place of the old chants!"

"He is an enthusiast, a fanatic. He has no sensibilities. He appeals for 'decision' in a single moment, and deludes the people into thinking they may *know* their sins are forgiven!"

Opposition increased, and the aristocracy and the rector found themselves on the same side as the rabble, whose way of living was openly condemned from the pulpit week after week. While the common people showed their hostility by open derision and sometimes persecution, the less vulgar folk followed a subtler way. They wrote to the ecclesiastical authorities and demanded episcopal restraint and punishment. The Bishops—Exeter, and Bath and Wells, who already had seen the promise of the young clergyman—were unwilling to interfere, and wrote remonstrances alike to Coke and his vicar.

It is surprising that Coke, on the one side, and the hostile faction, on the other, found it possible to live together in South Petherton for four years after his conversion. It was an uncomfortable period for both parties. There was too much that was likeable about the curate for the opposition to resort to open action, and Coke himself was unwilling to forsake the place where it seemed that God had sent him. By 1776, however, Coke's mind was turning to other places and wider possibilities.

A little earlier he had met a certain Mr. Brown, who had the double incumbency of Portishead, near Bristol, and Kingston, near Taunton. Like Coke's other guide, Maxfield, Brown was a friend of the Wesleys. He lent him two books of John Fletcher's to read. Fletcher, of Madeley, a clergyman who had never forsaken his parish to follow the Wesleys round about England on their preaching tours, but who had, nevertheless, both in his preaching and his writing been one of their staunchest fellow-workers, led Coke, through these books, as he had led many others, to a better understanding of the truths for which the Methodists stood. Coke began to feel he would like to meet John Wesley, if the opportunity came.

One day a message came from Mr. Brown. "Mr. Wesley is to stay with me at Taunton in August. Come and see him there."

On August 26th, 1776, Thomas Coke met John Wesley in Mr. Brown's garden. He had ridden twenty miles that day, and as soon as he began talking, and listening, to the old man he knew that the journey had been worth while. He knew, too, that the time had come to say farewell to his difficult charge at South Petherton, and that a new life was ahead of him.

He saw an old man of seventy-three, slim, vigorous in mind and commanding. His speech was forthright and he did not mince his words, but when he talked of spiritual things he spoke like a man who knew God. He certainly knew men. Coke had constantly to remind himself that this old man still rode thousands of miles every year, preached hundreds of times, began his day at four in the morning, was a notable writer and editor, was as well known in Ireland and Scotland and Wales as he was in England, where he was one of the best-known public figures of his age, and had an influence which extended on to the Continent and across the Atlantic to America. He knew that he was talking to the greatest man he had ever met.

Coke poured out his heart to the old man, there in the garden. He spoke of his conversion, of his difficulties, of his desire to serve the Church and his Lord, of his hopes for the future. Wesley, seeing the eagerness of the thirty-year-old Welshman, said little of the future and, in his usual cautious fashion, committed himself to nothing. He was interested and he was encouraging. But he made no offers, and did not appear to notice the young man's implicit appeal.

When he rode home, Coke was deflated and a little angry.

"I expected," he confided to his friends, "that he would have said, 'Come with me, and I will give you employment according to all that is in your heart'."

Wesley did nothing of the kind.

He told him to go back to South Petherton and conduct cottage-meetings amongst his degraded and evil-intentioned parishioners.

CHAPTER TWO

A PLAN FOR MISSIONS

Hogsheads of cider stood in the streets, with barrels of stones nearby. Slightly tipsy farmhands went from cottage to cottage, bellowing at those within to come out and join the fun. Slatternly women dragged ill-clad children towards the churchyard, where they sat on green, mossy gravestones, exchanging gossip, in their thick, west-country speech, with their neighbours. An air of excitement hung about the village. South Petherton was getting ready to enjoy itself.

Some of the men had blackthorn sticks swinging loosely in their hands, with which they cracked either at the cider barrels or passing cats and dogs. A mangy animal howled with pain as it tore down the street, its side ripped by a well-aimed stone. A loutish youth sped it with another stone.

"Save your powder for the doctor," ordered a man with a dirty wig, looking down from the heavily built horse he rode. He was obviously a ringleader, a highly placed servant in some local aristocrat's house.

"Here he comes!"

There was a sudden burst of discordant noise, high above their heads. The church bells began to clash and clang, without pattern or rhythm, and from the churchyard came an excited shouting, growing louder and rapidly nearer. The cries of the mob were taken up by the vicious crowd in the street, who grasped their sticks

tighter and thrust their hands into the barrels of stones.
Words came clearer.

"Turn him out."

"No Methodies here."

"He stopped the bull-baiting."

"He interferes with everyone's affairs."

"Give the Welshman a ducking, and cool him off."

Then, walking quickly, though not running, came
Coke. His hat had been knocked off, his preaching
bands were dragged under one ear, his gown was badly
torn and there was a cut on his cheek. Dignity, disappointment, anger and physical pain all fought for
possession of his mind, and he hardly noticed the stone
that whistled by his head and fell a little way in front.
A moment later he turned into his house, where the
windows were promptly broken by the mob, before they
surged back to broach the cider barrels and get drunk
at the expense of the local "lords of the manors" who
had provided the refreshment and incited the ruffians to
riot.

"This must be the end," thought Coke. The previous
Sunday had been bad; this was worse.

Following Wesley's advice, he had gone back to his
parish and modelled his work even more closely than he
had already done on the Methodist pattern. A plan of
preaching appointments was read out on Sundays from
the pulpit, cottage-meetings were begun and class-
meetings for fellowship and testimony started. The divi-
sion between the godly and the graceless in the village
was deepened, the hostility of the wealthy classes confirmed, and the rancour of his own employer, the vicar,
brought to such a point that he was given orders to
"get himself out of Somerset" and leave the village to
look after itself in peace.

Refusing to accept his dismissal, he preached and administered Communion the following Sunday, and was met by a mob when he left the church. The next week he tried again, was not allowed to enter the church, attempted to speak in the graveyard and was silenced by the clashing bells and threatened with violence if he did not go at once.

He went.

Where to go, he had no idea. He had no desire for the life represented by Brecon and its society, and little, at this moment, for the honours of the greater Church offices. He believed that, if he had been allowed to remain in South Petherton a little longer, he might have done much good for the village and gained some advancement himself, but, nevertheless, his great ambition was to win men and women for God. *That* could be done wherever he was. Though Wesley had sent him back to his curacy, no doubt to test his sincerity of purpose, he had learned much from him in the hours they spent together in Taunton, and not least that a man's work is wherever he is.

Wesley . . . What would Wesley say now, he wondered, after he had been turned out of his parish?

What Wesley said was simple, no more than a twisting of the phrases of his own motto, but it dominated the whole of Thomas Coke's life from that moment onwards.

The old evangelist was not surprised when Coke sought him out. "A union has begun," he wrote after he had first met him at Taunton, "which I trust shall never end." Nor was he surprised that the eager young doctor of civil law had antagonised his parishioners and been thrust out. He did not intend to give him any further testing of the kind he had gone through.

"I have no parish, no church, Mr. Wesley," stated Coke. "What shall I do?"

"Why," answered the old man, taking both of Coke's hands between his own thin palms, "go and preach the gospel to all the world."

It was perhaps no more than a turn of speech to John Wesley. Though he spoke of the world being his parish he travelled about it less than Whitefield, from whom he borrowed the expression. He went only once to America and, though he moved incessantly about England and Wales, he had little love for the continent of Europe. In his assessment of what should be attempted and what might reasonably be done, he was one of the most practical men who have ever controlled a great religious movement. England needed converting to God; Wales and Ireland and Scotland were largely unevangelised. The work of the Methodist preachers was quite clearly defined for a long time to come. Undoubtedly America would soon be raising new problems, after the war was ended, but they could be faced when they came. Meanwhile older helpers were falling out, new ones were not always reliable; his brother Charles, becoming less adventurous and in some ways less sympathetic, was itinerating but little, and leaders such as Fletcher, for the most part, had had their days of influence and power. Here, at his side, stood an earnest, charming, young man of ability and force of character, the very man to replace some of those who were giving up the work. Wesley had no doubt of his powers, though Coke combined a certain self-esteem and evident ambition with them.

"Join us," he invited. "We can use you amongst us in these days. There is much work to do. Go and preach the gospel—to all the world."

In Wesley's mind there was no thought of India,

Africa, China or the South Seas. Britain and perhaps, from a distance, America were all the world he could encompass. To Coke, even at that moment, it was different. As they rode towards Bristol together a lady of fashion passed them in her carriage, with a small negro boy perched high on the box by the driver. Wherever they went, in town or in country house, they came across such dark-skinned folk, occasionally pampered like pet spaniels, but not infrequently turned out as useless to die or forage for a living as best they could. Had not Mr. Wesley himself told the story more than once, thought Coke, of how—twenty years earlier —he had preached in Wandsworth, in the house of Mr. Nathaniel Gilbert, to three such black slaves who were by that service soundly converted from their dreadful paganism to God? And was not Mr. Gilbert, the Speaker of the House of Assembly in the West Indian island of Antigua, a leader amongst those who ministered to such negro slaves in his own island?

Coke's mind was already far away. "To all the world." He day-dreamed, he saw visions and believed in what he saw, he planned great enterprises on a foundation of hope and desire. He saw those who had never heard of Christ bowing at His name. He saw America . . . Africa . . . India . . . Ceylon. He saw ships . . . palm-trees . . . jungles . . . crowds. His mind ranged everywhere, led on from one lovely picture to another. He saw Methodism, of which he was not yet even a part, committed to its founder's axiom, the world its parish. Wherever he looked he found hope and possibility, a ready welcome and a glad response.

Wherever he looked, too, whether in Africa or India, on shipboard or in the jungle, in Methodist councils or missionary advance, he saw himself, Dr. Thomas Coke, in the centre of the picture. He was not conscious of being ambitious. Knowing his own ability, though never deliberately falling back either on his charm or his power, it was perfectly natural to him that he should be the leader rather than the led, the one who rose whoever else might fall.

The pre-eminence he saw for himself, it should be noted, was only within a limited and maligned community. Methodism was not England, and in joining the Methodists Coke was turning his back on general popularity and ecclesiastical advancement. Wesley wrote that the young man "had bid adieu to his honourable name," and Coke himself spoke of "the despised people called Methodists, among whom I am determined to live and die."

In that comparatively limited sphere, dominated by the personality and the judgment of John Wesley, and, despite its closely knit and zealous membership, not infrequently stirred by personal irritations and resentments, Thomas Coke's rise to power was sudden, swift and not universally welcome.

He joined Wesley in 1777 and the next year his name first appeared on the list of stations of the preachers. He was appointed to London, standing third to John Wesley himself in the list of ministers there. Wesley neither accepted nor acted upon criticisms when he felt himself in the right, and though, from the first, there was resentment against the appointment, Wesley knew he had a man who could help him by more than preaching.

Even as a preacher he was an asset to the staff of the London circuit. The old Foundery in Moorfields, where Methodism began, was becoming more and more out of date, and Coke, appointed to minister there, took to the fields and—though he was without Wesley's devastating logic or Whitefield's thundering passion, being a man of simple, biblical, homely phrases and far-from-powerful voice—gathered thousands about him on the open space near where Tavistock Square now stands.

Wesley needed a competent secretary, who could carry out his wishes and occasionally act on his own initiative, though in accordance with the old man's principles, even more than he needed a new preacher in London. For the five years that followed his appointment to London Coke served as the great man's assistant and representative. He wrote innumerable letters and travelled thousands of miles on the most diverse matters.

Sometimes he is insisting that the moneys from the burial-ground at City Road are for the expenses of the "house steward" there. Then he issues orders for the renewal of a gallery, likely to fall, in a church where Wesley is shortly to preach and there are certain to be crowds—and a critical eye for detail. Again, he is demanding a rail in an Exeter chapel to separate men and women, or riding to Bath to compose differences in the society.

Such work and travel brought him constantly before Methodist people everywhere. Soon his name was known throughout the country, and he gained interest, much as Wesley had done earlier, because of his Oxford traditions and intellectual brilliance.

To be well known was not necessarily to be popular, however, and two issues, both initiated by Wesley, added to Coke's difficulties.

The first was in 1782, when Wesley sent him to Ireland to gather together the first Conference of the Methodist preachers there, and to preside over it as the Founder's representative. Although there were some who felt this honour to be too high and too quickly achieved, most of the preachers were ready to wish him well and, from the day he arrived there, Ireland took him to her heart. Several years later—he presided over the Irish Conference almost every year to the end of his life—they wrote, "Our love and respect for him increase every year, so that we are ready to look upon ourselves as orphans when contrary winds delay his coming."

Less easily acceptable was the part he played in drawing up the "Deed of Declaration." Wesley saw death becoming more imminent and was concerned about what would happen to Methodism afterwards. He had devolved much of the administrative government upon the Conference, but retained the power of veto. The Conference had no legal power and, when Wesley's authority was gone, trustees might feel themselves free to do whatever they liked with their buildings or their preachers. Coke's legal knowledge, good though it was, was not sufficient to produce such a document as Wesley needed, but it was enough to put him on terms with Wesley's lawyer, Clulow, and the eminent King's Counsel, Maddox, who finally drew up a legal document by which the control of Methodism was vested in one hundred preachers who were therein named, and amongst whom vacancies should be filled by election. One hundred was almost exactly half of the number of preachers in Methodism. Of the half who were left out, every one could see reasons for his own inclusion, reasons against the choosing of someone else, and reasons for maligning Coke, who, it was generally presumed, had submitted the list to Wesley.

Wesley had chosen his own list, uninfluenced by anyone, and made that quite plain, but for a long time there were those who used the occasion as an opportunity for undermining Coke's growing influence.

It was greatly to the credit of the real leaders amongst the preachers that such men as Samuel Bradburn and Joseph Benson—whom he charged quite falsely with heresy just after his entry into Methodism—accepted him in friendship and brotherliness. Wesley wrote to a friend in Brecon, Coke's own birthplace, that the young man "promises fair, and gives us reason to hope that he will bring forth not only blossom, but fruit. He seems to be aware of his own great enemy, applause."

Coke, however, was no mere legally minded secretary. He was an evangelist, who could not lose the urgent desire to save souls in the business of writing letters. The evangelistic passion which aroused South Petherton to mob violence, won converts and enemies wherever he travelled. In Ramsbury, in Wiltshire, he was assaulted with sticks and stones, had his gown torn from his back and was drenched from the fire-engine. They shouted "False prophet" after him when he warned them they might need their fire-engine sooner than they thought, and fell into superstitious fear when part of the village was burnt down the following week. In Stafford, dining at an inn with two preachers who were going to Macclesfield, he borrowed a table from the landlord, sent the bellman round the town to announce that Dr. Thomas Coke, of Oxford, was to preach in the market-place and had formed a small group of converted people into a society almost before he had left on his travels.

Yet, whatever he was doing and wherever he preached, the words of Wesley's first greeting rang in his ears: "Go and preach the gospel to all the world."

It was not enough to make converts in Stafford or

Bath or Petherton, where he was welcomed by a repentant people when he returned to preach. The negro slaves and servants were a constant reproach. To Coke, "all the world" meant the world and not England, or even England, Ireland, Scotland and Wales. His very successes in Britain made it all the more imperative to remember those who had had no opportunity of hearing the gospel.

In addition, he was in correspondence with one or two like-minded people in Britain and abroad. He met soldiers who had fought in India and amongst the Mohammedans, and heard their accounts of heathenism. He corresponded with a Government servant in Bengal, Mr. Charles Grant, later to rise high in Indian affairs, about the possibility of a mission in India, and especially in Bengal. He learned from the Moravians, to whom John and Charles Wesley owed so much, about their missions in America, in the West Indies and in Asia.

He stayed with a barrister, Thomas Parker, at York, and talked far into the night.

In January 1784 he looked critically and hopefully at a little circular which had just been published. It was addressed "to all the real lovers of mankind," and was signed by himself and Thomas Parker. It asked for subscriptions of two guineas a year, and bore the names of twenty-five contributors, Coke himself heading the list. It had a simple, straightforward title:

A Plan of the Society for the Establishment of Missions Among the Heathen.

For the first time the people called Methodists had the claims of an unevangelised world set before them. They, and others besides "who are entirely unconnected with the Methodists and are determined so to be," were asked for money and interest. The Society, out of these funds, proposed to pay the passages, the cost of language instruction and the living expenses of missionaries or other civil employees whom it deemed fit. It also desired to print and distribute the Scriptures in other tongues "for the use of any heathen country."

Just over six years after Coke's entry into Methodism he had begun to commit it to its most romantic and adventurous undertaking and to pledge himself to his lifework.

It was a little over two years later that another pioneer, William Carey, made his great appeal to the Baptist Church.

CHAPTER THREE

LAND OF THE FREE
(1784–1792)

JOHN WESLEY'S correspondence was large and its subjects various. He dealt with the reasons for the failure of the work in Edinburgh, the difficulties of the preacher's finances in Exeter, the demands of his London printers, the scurrilous attacks of his vilifiers in the Press, one after the other with, apparently, equal interest and care. Occasionally he found in his letters an account of some strange happening which fascinated him enough for him to record it in his *Journal*—a ghostly appearance, a dream, a death-bed scene. Once, at least, such an account of a passing dream was worth preserving in print. A lady wrote to tell him she had dreamed she was in a large church, with a great congregation, waiting for the preacher. She knew they were, in fact, waiting for Mr. Wesley. Suddenly there was a stirring of the people and she looked round to find a coffin being borne into the church—Mr. Wesley's coffin. Before it, in mourning, representing the Methodist people, walked the Rev. John Fletcher and Dr. Thomas Coke.

Wesley's reception of the "prophecy" was somewhat cold, but interested. He must have been impressed by the thought of Coke walking as chief mourner with Fletcher, for Coke supplied exactly those qualities of optimism, resilience and encouragement which Fletcher, of Madeley, had given to Methodism in its early days.

Even more interesting is the fact that Methodism generally put so high an estimate on the worth of the impetuous little Welshman.

It was with the clear knowledge of his habit of speaking and acting first, when his heart was moved, and thinking afterwards, that Wesley chose him for the most important task he had ever delegated to anyone in Methodism. Wesley knew the dangers of putting responsibility in Coke's hands. "The doctor is often too hasty. He does not always consider all the circumstances"—so he wrote to a mutual friend. He knew that his mind was, even at this time, apt to be carried away on flights of fancy to the ends of the earth, with sad results to the immediate task. "The doctor is apt to forget," he complained to his brother Charles. He gave a delayed assent to Coke's *Plan for Missions,* though he regarded the whole scheme as both impracticable and of secondary importance just then. He knew with what ease Coke mixed with ordinary people in town and country, and how they valued him, but at the same time he looked askance at his courtliness and aristocratic charm, and reproved him for too great a liking for "the nobility." Wesley, despite his own ancestry and bearing, was seldom at ease with the rich and worldly; Coke, on the other hand, found himself at home amongst them, and it was as well, on some later occasions, that he had such ready access to them.

Coke, in 1784, longed for a way to be opened for a mission to the East. He hoped that he might even be able to go himself.

Wesley, in the same year, put the matter aside. He thought of America, the land of the newly free.

Methodism had been introduced to America by Irishmen, for Strawbridge, who preached first in Maryland, was a native of County Leitrim, and Philip Embury, who began the work in New York, was a German émigré from Limerick. The earliest preaching-places had been the homes of the people, a barn, and a loft used for storing ships' rigging. From the beginning, Methodism grew rapidly under its simple but (like Captain Thomas Webb with his patched eye, brilliant regimentals and bared sword) occasionally picturesque pioneers. In 1769 the first two "missionaries" were sent by the Methodist Conference, in response to appeals from America for help, and the British Press satirised the Wesleys, dubbing them the Bishops of Pennsylvania and Nova Scotia. Two years later the greatest of all Methodism's sons to go to America volunteered for the work. Francis Asbury was a young man who, before his death, was to ride hundreds of thousands of miles preaching the gospel and establishing Methodism throughout the Continent. Wesley sent him, unordained as he was, to preach and do what work he could.

Four years afterwards the Americans, irritated beyond endurance by the taxation, the irresponsibility and the high-handedness of the British Government, rebelled and fought actions with the British Army at Lexington and Concord. They had determined to be free of control exercised without knowledge from a capital thousands of miles overseas. Their only asset was the will to win, for they were little more than a rabble in arms, and poorly armed at that. Nevertheless, in 1776, they issued a "Declaration of Independence," and somehow the fight went on.

Methodism was in a difficult position. Wesley, a High Church Tory, was thoroughly out of sympathy with the rebellious colonists and inflamed them with a pamphlet which he had the cynical temerity to call *A Calm Address to our American Colonies.* Several of the Methodist preachers were known to be loyalists and brought the Society into disrepute with the colonial leaders by distributing copies of Wesley's tract and the King's *Proclamation.* Some were even discovered to be involved in plots with the British against the Americans. They were dangerous times, and those whose sympathies were against the rebels were wise to leave the country.

It is strange to think that the whole of North America at this time was a part of the Diocese of London. The Bishop of London had no interest in people who rejected his country's supremacy and his own episcopal wisdom, and when most of the clergy returned—hardly one was left in America when the Declaration of Independence was signed—he did nothing to replace them.

The result was that, in 1783, when the colonists had decisively beaten the British armies and forced them to withdraw, and had passed a resolution declaring hostilities at an end, there were no clergy left in America, except those who had associations with Scandinavia or Germany or other parts of the Continent. For the most part, the citizens of the prairies and the backwoods, and even many of the towns, had no one to marry them, no one to baptise them, no one to bury them and no one to administer the sacrament of Holy Communion. Methodism had not a single ordained clergyman in the continent, and the once-established Church of England was dead.

The cry for help came over the water. Wesley went to the Bishop of London and was rebuffed; he wrote to John Moore, Archbishop of Canterbury, "the most sordid ecclesiastical nepotist of his nepotic century," with the same result.

The cry came again. And again.

Wesley had no mind to desert the people of America, whether he agreed or disagreed with their politics. George III said to the representative of the new nation at his court, "I was the last man in the Kingdom to acknowledge your independence and I will be the last to violate it." Wesley knew he must do more than accept the new position; he must take some part in it.

In February 1784, the month after Coke published his *Plan for Missions,* he was summoned by Wesley to discuss, as he was told, a matter of the most urgent importance. When he parted from the old man his usually cheerful, red face was solemn and a little shocked.

He turned back to repeat his last words. "I cannot even consider it. I must absolutely refuse."

As usual, he thought again after he had spoken. Two months later he wrote to Wesley to say that he had changed his mind.

On September 2nd an event took place in Bristol of the utmost significance for the future of American Methodism, and which finally caused the severance of Methodism from the Church of England in Britain. On that day, probably at number 6, Dighton Street, John Wesley laid his hands on Richard Whatcoat and Thomas Vasey, nominating them as "presbyters," and on Thomas Coke, designating him "superintendent" of the work in America. In everything but the use of the term itself it was ordination.

Wesley's suggestion had been simple, and, to himself, theologically sound as well as practically defensible. The American people must not be left without benefit of clergy, or they would suffer greatly, be led into breaches of church discipline far more serious than that which he contemplated, and perhaps inevitably into open sin and immorality. If the bishops would not ordain men to go to America, then he would risk every certain consequence of his action, and do so himself. As this would be merely a temporary and local relief, he proposed to "set aside" Coke and charge him with the responsibility of ordaining Francis Asbury, if Asbury agreed. Coke's visit to America would be short, Asbury would remain there. Coke's "superintendency" would be nominal, Asbury's real, for he was already, in the minds of the American people, the head of the Methodist Church there.

Coke objected at first. Later he wrote and admitted that, as there was need of a man with influence and prudence, and as he could lay claim to the first quality if not the second, he would consider the matter. Finally, with his mind full of plans and dreams, he agreed and accepted the laying-on of Wesley's hands before sailing for America with Whatcoat and Vasey in September.

They left behind a turmoil in Methodism and much abuse outside of it. Charles Wesley was furiously angry. He penned a satirical quatrain:

"Since bishops are so easy made
By man or woman's whim,
Wesley his hands on Coke hath laid,
But who laid hands on him?"

John replied, swiftly and concisely. "If you will not or cannot help me, do not hinder those who will. I must and will save as many souls as I can while I live, without being careful of what may possibly be when I die."

Coke was too busy thinking about the future to care, either, what might possibly be when he returned. He was going to a new country, to share in its beginnings. He was in an ocean-going ship for the first time in his life. He might meet the leaders of the Revolution; he would certainly get to know the leaders of the Church. He was a man of authority, heading for adventure, and whatever he did was bound to affect the future of the United States. It was a task immensely to his liking.

He talked, wrote, read and watched everything with eager interest. He meditated on his own position, and read Bishop Hoadley on *Orders*. He dreamed of the United States, recalled the disastrous experiments of the Wesleys there in the 1730's, wondered if he would have a chance of preaching to the Red Indians and read the *Life of David Brainerd*. He read the Bible in Greek and Hebrew, and Virgil and Augustine in Latin. He made notes of storms, whales and porpoises, and wrote reflectively of dolphin that it was "more like salmon than any fish I ever tasted."

On November 3rd, 1784, he landed in New York.

The next six months were almost exhaustingly full of interest.

He stayed, with Whatcoat and Vasey, for his first night in America, at the home of Stephen Sands, a New York Methodist. He saw the bustling harbour, the busy traffic of the town. Its buildings were still damaged, in some cases, but "Wesley's Chapel" stood upright enough. He noticed there were neither British soldiers nor Red Indians, though there were plenty of Germans and Scandinavians. The deportment of the people was steady and solid, rather than proud or arrogant, and their speech was sober, with a smacking of the puritan in word and dress. They wore victory and freedom easily, and welcomed Coke with ready friendliness.

That same night John Dickens, the preacher in New York, came to supper and talked with the three new-comers and their host about Wesley's scheme. They were surprised at its audacity but felt there was every reason for accepting it. There was less difficulty in breaking with ecclesiastical tradition now that they had broken with political supremacy in Britain. They, and all whom Coke talked with later, were aware of the foolishness of expecting primates and bishops in the safe sinecures of England to understand the needs of a scattered, isolated community undergoing the rigours and disasters of a pioneering life. If John Wesley had initiated such a scheme, Dickens assured Coke that there was every reason to hope the American preachers would put it into action.

"Mr. Asbury is in Maryland. You had best ride south to meet him," Coke was told.

A few days later he set off for the south, preaching as he went. The country was fascinating, with its tremendous forests, its tiny hamlets, its ready if limited hospitality, and wherever he went he found a welcome. He loved the American people from the first moment he came amongst them, for they had something of his own adventurous, undefeatable spirit and optimism.

At last he came to Barrett's Chapel, in Maryland, set in a clearing of the forest. There, to a full congregation in the rough-hewn seats, with the first snow weighing down the branches of the overhanging trees, he spoke of the love of God. At the end of the service a plain, robust man walked up the aisle and into the pulpit. He looked like a horseman, pausing to worship before he continued his journey. He put his arms about Coke's shoulders and kissed his cheek in greeting.

"You are Mr. Asbury?" the preacher surmised.

"I am, sir. And I welcome you to America in the name of the Lord."

"I have been seeking you," said Coke. "I bring you

very urgent news from Mr. Wesley. When can we talk together?"

They talked then, and thenceforward for hours. At first Asbury was shocked by the proposal, though it did not take him long to see the value of the scheme. His own position was clear, though the visitor's was less so. For his part he could do nothing, accept nothing, whatever Wesley might say, which was not the wish of the American preachers over whom he would have authority.

Before they parted they had drawn up an itinerary for Coke in the next few weeks (there is reason to think that the rough-riding Asbury was determined to test the staying-power of the charming doctor of law); arranged for the preachers to be called together at Christmas to discuss the proposals; talked of the future policy of the Church and Conference, should the preachers agree; and worked out plans for a school or college, with several possible sites. From the first, Asbury and Coke were friends.

Freeborn Garrettson, the son of a man of wealth and influence, who felt the call of God so strongly that in his own words he "flung the reins of the bridle across the horse's neck and, folding my hands, cried out, 'Lord, I submit,'" and had soon afterwards joined the ranks of the Methodist preachers, was sent off from the north to the south. As he went, "like an arrow" as he said, he sent messengers to right and left summoning the preachers to Baltimore on Christmas Eve.

Before that time Coke had ridden a thousand miles in the eastern states. Forests full of snow, forests on fire, forests haunted by stealthy Redskins; churches half full at five in the morning, churches where there had been no baptisms for ten years, churches whose doors were locked against him; hospitable sheriffs and kindly innkeepers, reluctant hosts and angry enemies; a ride of twenty-five miles to a church he could not see for the trees and an additional ride of eighteen miles to circle back to it, half drowning in a flooded river on the way—all these are recorded in a fully stocked diary.

Then came Baltimore. Out of eighty-one preachers in America sixty were gathered there to discuss the new project in Lovely Lane Chapel on Christmas Day. They stayed with Henry Dorsey Gough, at Perry Hall, one of the largest and noblest houses in America, and, lodged in comfort, they talked over the scheme.

The next day there was comparatively little discussion. The Christmas Conference was unanimous in its love for Asbury, its acceptance of his supremacy, its desire for his ordination and its respect for Wesley's messenger, Thomas Coke. In drab coats, large waistcoats, plain stocks, with no gowns or bands, their broad-brimmed, low-crowned hats by their sides, they voted and prayed as one man.

Two days later, with the assistance of a German minister, Coke ordained Asbury as "superintendent" of the Methodist Church in America.

Not so far away, General Washington discussed the preceedings of the Conference, read Coke's plain, simple sermon and put it on his library shelves.

For another six months Coke rode through the United States, preaching, talking, making friends and gaining a deeper and more permanent regard for these stout freemen. He found wearisome a consistent diet of eggs and bacon for weeks, at breakfast and supper, but appreciated the hospitality of the forest-dwellers as much as he liked that of the Governor of Philadelphia, whom he discovered to be a friend of John Fletcher and an admirer of the Wesleys. Towards June he planned the site of a college near Baltimore, and agreed to its being named, in his own honour and Asbury's, Cokesbury College.

He returned to Britain in a state of exultation. He had done what he was expected to do, and more. He was so full of America that he had almost forgotten, for the time being, his plan to send missionaries to the East.

This was the first of many visits. He returned to America as the accredited representative of the British Conference, and the fellow-superintendent of the work there with Asbury, in 1787, 1788, 1790 and 1792. There were more visits after that, but by that date Coke had opened himself to severe criticism amongst his brethren in Britain, and especially by John Wesley.

In a very short time the American Methodists referred to themselves as an "Episcopal" Church, and in this they were not unreasonable. In 1887 they referred to Asbury as a bishop. Two years later they honoured the irate Wesley with the same title, and in 1792 Coke and Asbury both spoke easily of themselves as bishops.

Wesley wrote in furious horror: "How can you, how dare you suffer yourself to be called a Bishop? I shudder, I start, at the very thought! Men may call me a knave or a fool, a rascal, a scoundrel, and I am content; but they shall never, by my consent, call me Bishop! End this!" He wrote, too, "I found a school; you found a college! More, you call it by your own names! I think you magnify yourselves!"

What he said to Coke, whom he could see—this old, brilliant autocrat, who had ruled Methodism more rigidly, if more lovingly, than any bishop or archbishop had authority to do amongst his own people— must have been more sharp and incisive than anything he wrote to Asbury, over the water. Before his death Wesley saw clearly the danger of any other man rising to the position he held in Methodism, and would not tolerate—any more than a restive Conference would permit—a successor to his own authority.

Coke, however, well pleased with all he had seen and done in America on his first visit, reporting at first hand on the strange results of the war, during which Methodism had grown in numbers and spiritual power, despite all the persecution to which it had been subjected, had no mind to seek authority or influence. He was full of America, full of delight at the way the gospel was spreading, full of plans for wider work and a greater kingdom yet for his Lord.

Could not something now be done to implement his *Plan for Missions*? What about Africa?

Wesley was adamant. Africa could wait. On Coke's own showing America had the first claim on men, and prayer, and money.

CHAPTER FOUR

CHRISTMAS DAY
(1786–1788)

On September 24th, 1786, Coke set sail again.

Since he returned from America he had been engaged in preaching-tours round England, in visiting Ireland and presiding over the Conference there, and in a great deal of routine work. Wesley was turned eighty, and not disposed to discuss plans for work in the East when, as he clearly saw, so much needed yet to be done in the West. Coke, the ardent enthusiast for missions to the heathen, by his actions in America and his own encouragement to the preachers there to hope for recruits from the English Conference, had made it unlikely that his plan for missions in the East would be supported. Such "missionaries" as volunteered to go overseas, separating from their homeland and their families, were promised to America for work in the remote areas of Newfoundland, Nova Scotia and the like. One, however, had been sought for the West Indian island of Antigua, where a certain John Baxter had been "set apart" as elder, and had given up his civil occupation to devote himself to the work of the ministry.

Coke set off, on what was perhaps the most significant of all his voyages, with William Warrener, who was to be sent from America to Antigua, and William Hammit and John Clarke, who were to be stationed in Nova Scotia. The ship was bound for America.

From the beginning the voyage was disastrous. The

ship beat into the wind round the Kent coast and was driven towards the shore, so that Coke, who had been wondering where he would preach his first sermon on land again, found himself preaching in Portsmouth instead of New York. They nearly ran into a sloop, and narrowly escaped being run down by a frigate off Land's End, and rejoiced when at last they saw the open sea beyond the Irish coast. Rejoicing was soon turned to anxiety, and anxiety, once or twice, almost to despair. Contrary winds drove them farther and farther out of their course, tore at the rigging and the sails, and drove great seas against the tiny vessel. A hole was burst in the side of the ship which it took all the skill of the company to mend, day after day; and the rigging was torn away from the mainmast, so that they drove at the mercy of the storm. Food began to run short, and they were almost without water by the time they had been at sea for two months. On his first voyage Coke had reached America in six weeks; this time, after three months, with Christmas approaching, they were many hundreds of miles away from the mainland. The captain who, with the crew, had all the illiterate seaman's horror of parsons aboard a sailing-ship, grew more and more morose and revengeful.

"Throw the Jonahs overboard!"

The demand gathered strength, and captain and crew burst into the ministers' cabin, tore up their papers, thrust their books into the sea and beat Coke and his companions about the head while they tried to drag them towards the ship's side. Either their better senses returned or they felt sufficiently relieved of their spite, for they left the bruised passengers alone, all of a sudden, and returned to their work below decks.

A little while before Christmas the captain determined

to run for the West Indies, since there was no hope of making the American ports, and food and water were practically gone. On Christmas Eve the look-out sighted a grey streak of land on the horizon, and by dark it was possible to see the lights of a town. Just after midnight they touched the wharf and, in the early hours of the morning, Coke and his three companions left the battered ship, to their own relief and that of their blasphemous fellow-travellers, and set out along the road into the town.

Round the corner came a man with a lantern. In a second or two they met.

"I understand this is the island of Antigua," said Coke, and the stranger nodded. "We have just arrived from England, having been driven far off our course. My name is Coke. . . ."

The stranger, whom they now saw to be wearing the dress of a preacher, lifted his lantern towards their faces. His delight was too great for words.

"And I am John Baxter, of English Harbour," he announced. "I am on my way to conduct Christmas morning worship. You must come with me. And, of course, you must preach to us. But first you will need refreshment." He led them away to his house, all talking, questioning, at the same time.

It seemed a strange chance that had driven the missionary-minded Coke, with his passion for work amongst the negroes and Asiatics, to the little island of Antigua.

In 1758 John Wesley preached to the Gilbert family in Wandsworth, "a desolate spot." He saw three slaves amongst the company. A little while later they were baptised. That action was the kindling of a flame which was to sweep the West Indies with fire. Richard Gilbert,

Road in Antigua where Coke and Baxter probably met.

a medical graduate of Cambridge, had been introduced
to Methodism before he went to practise as a doctor in
the West Indies. He chose the island where his brother
Nathaniel was a landed gentleman and Speaker of the
House of Assembly, Antigua, and, some time after he
arrived, tried to interest him in Methodism. Nathaniel
had no time and little interest in the subject, until one
day he was taken with a fever and had to remain in bed.
Sending for a certain book to read, he found he had
been brought, by mistake, a copy of John Wesley's
Earnest Appeal to Men of Reason and Religion, which his
brother had left behind. The pamphlet made so strong
an impression on his mind that he determined to come
to England specially to meet the author, and Wesley's
visit to Wandsworth was the result.

From that time forward the Gilberts were devoted to
the work of Methodism. Nathaniel opened his house for
services, which he conducted himself, and to which he
took the daring course of inviting the negro slaves, and
later gave up his appointment under the Government
and laboured entirely as a lay preacher. His brother and
his family and servants all joined in the work and, by
1773, fifteen years after his first meeting with Wesley,
there was a large Methodist community on the island.
Fortunately the relationships of masters and slaves had
always been better in Antigua than in any other of the
West Indian islands, so the work was not greatly hindered by persecution or prejudice.

In 1773 Nathaniel Gilbert died and his brother had
to return to England because of ill-health. The work
was left to a couple of negresses, and, despite their
devotion, it is not surprising that it flagged. There was a
great difference, even to black slaves—and much more
to their white masters—in Methodism led by a planta-

tion owner, and in services conducted by plantation workers.

Five years later a shipwright was appointed to English Harbour, Antigua, named John Baxter. His friends dissuaded him from accepting the appointment but, largely on the advice of John Wesley, he went. He was no mere labourer, for his salary, even in those days of low wages and prices, was four hundred pounds a year, and he found ready entrance to many of the good homes of the island. More than shipbuilding, however, had attracted him to the harbour where Rodney, Hood and Nelson were to refit their ships; he had heard of the needs of the island Methodists, and set himself out, immediately after his arrival, to serve them. A year later there were six hundred members, and in 1784 the Conference which Coke had attended at Baltimore, where Asbury was ordained, had set Baxter apart for work in Antigua. As a result he had given up his trade as a shipwright, sacrificed a large income and set himself to work amongst the black immigrants of the island. The previous year he had built, with money from influential whites and labour from the blacks, a spacious church, the first Methodist building in the West Indies.

It was this man whom Coke and his friends met on Christmas Day, 1786.

At five o'clock Coke, his mind for the moment dead to America and full of his missionary dreams once more, entered the church. He faced the strangest congregation he had ever seen, yet a congregation that had haunted his dream for years. He saw two thousand negroes, almost all slaves, clean, well-behaved, the women dressed in white linen gowns, petticoats and caps, and the men, in their drabber fashion, as neat as the women.

It was one of the greatest moments of his life.

John Wesley, thinking of the storms, had dreamed of the doctor coming to him in the night with a pale face and wet clothes and hair. He had prayed, during the storm, that he might reach America safely and quickly. But disasters are used, in the providence of God, to effect new triumphs, and no one in England had any idea of the news Coke was to bring home with him a few months later. Wesley had written in his neat hand: "Wm. Hammit and Jn. Clarke, Nova Scotia." Coke, as he looked at this Christmas congregation, made up his mind while he preached that the men who were designated for America must stay in the West Indies.

If he could neither go nor send to the East nor to Africa, then *this* should be Methodism's first missionary enterprise. Indeed, it was that already.

For two months he remained in the West Indies, preaching, planning and touring.

While he was in Antigua he preached twice every day. It was not often that the island had the honour of an Oxford doctor of laws, with such charming manners and personable appearance. He looked more the gentleman than the parson, thought the planters, and invited him and, as a courtesy, his friends to dine and sup throughout the island. His black hair, his flashing eye and his soft Welsh voice captivated his hearers, so that the preaching-house was constantly filled with aristocratic people, and the poor slaves had to make what room they could for themselves in the back of the room.

So delighted were his hosts that one gentleman, whom he met when dining with the admiral of the fleet, who was later to become King William IV, offered him £500 a year if he would take a living in Antigua. Coke's reply was characteristic. "God be praised," he said, "five hundred thousand a year would be to me but a feather, when opposed to my usefulness in the Church of Christ."

Nothing—neither reward nor opposition nor sickness —would ever detain him long in one place. He must be about his business, hurrying, driven by deep desire, never at rest.

In the two months that followed his arrival in Antigua he saw much of the islands nearby, being taken by Baxter on a tour of those within easy reach. He wanted to see every corner of his new field, to take note of the work that was going on, to assess the needs of the islands and to decide where to station his two remaining men. Warrener remained in Antigua to help Baxter.

The islands had been one of the battlefields for the French and British navies, and the engagements of the armies in Canada and India, which had long ceased, were continued in the island channels until three or four years before Coke's arrival, for the French had used their fleet to aid the American "rebels" in their war of independence.

As they left Antigua, Coke was reminded that the discovery of many of the islands was due to Christopher Columbus. Antigua itself had been named by him after the church of Santa Maria la Antigua, in Seville. The first great island they reached, Dominica, he had so called because they discovered it on "the Master's day," Sunday. St. Vincent was sighted on the day sacred to that saint in the Spanish calendar, and St. Kitt's, an abbreviation of St. Christopher's, was given the name of his own patron saint. Spanish names, French traditions, Dutch language—all were found in the islands.

As they passed Dominica the sailors told of how De Grasse, the French admiral, had been beaten there in the channel by Admiral Rodney. St. Vincent had fallen into

British hands less than three years previously, and St. Kitts had seen the already defeated De Grasse beaten again, this time by Admiral Hood.

Coke, however interested he was in all this information, was far more intent on other things.

How many churches were there on the island of Dominica? What chance was there of settling a missionary there? Perhaps, after all, it would be better to press on to an island where the French were less strongly entrenched and Catholicism not the prevalent faith.

What about St. Vincent? He was shocked beyond measure to find that the island had a population of thirty thousand people, divided into four parishes—and that there was but one clergyman on the island, who did nothing more effective than conduct an occasional service in the court-house at Kingston for a few white settlers. No wonder the blacks to whom Coke preached were overheard to say: "This man has been imported for our benefit." They found a ready welcome amongst whites, too. In the interior a barn was set aside and, when they returned to the capital, they discovered that a wealthy gentleman had purchased a disused warehouse and fitted it up as a chapel.

Here was an obvious place for one of the missionaries to remain, and Clarke was left behind.

Hammit stayed at St. Kitts, where there was an almost equal need and just as great a welcome.

A situation of a different kind was discovered at the Dutch island of St. Eustatius. Here war had made a welcome unlikely. The island had been neutral and, in addition, a free port during the war, and thus had been largely used by French and Americans to gather equipment for the colonists' armies. The Dutch sympathies were clearly with the Americans, however, and British patience was tried by their attitude. When a shore battery fired a salute as a ship bearing the rebel flag drew into the harbour, the British admiral Rodney made the error an excuse for sweeping down on the island, firing part of the town and commandeering the one hundred and fifty vessels lying in the harbour as prizes of war. The British were unpopular, to say the least.

Coke found himself under orders not to preach until he had satisfied the authorities about his creed and his means of livelihood. His words had to be translated by an interpreter, though most of the islanders understood English, and he was given little encouragement during the few days he remained under surveillance on the island. He was permitted to preach once or twice to the negro slaves and left them in the care of one of their number, Black Harry.

This was almost his last stop in the islands before he set off, alone, for America.

On his return he reported to a deeply moved Conference that there were not only twenty-five thousand Methodists in America, but almost three thousand in the West Indies, mostly slaves, and that, whatever the relationship of the Conference to America might eventually become, Methodism had a mission-field which would constantly tax its resources, and give it much rejoicing, in the West Indian islands.

CHAPTER FIVE

WEST INDIAN WANDERER
(1788–1802)

COKE'S whole self was radiant as he told the Conference of what he had found and done in the West Indies, and as the preachers listened they caught something of the glow and fire that burned in the speaker. He had, on his own authority, stationed men in the islands whom Conference had designated for America, he had pledged the Conference to fuller support still—and the Conference, always a little restive under any suggestion of usurped authority, and by no means convinced that it should be persuaded into embarking on missionary ventures in the East, gave its whole-hearted applause to Coke's actions and promises. They found themselves committed to something which would grow out of all knowledge and make tremendous demands on the patience and service of them all, and they rejoiced to see the work beginning. Whether they would have agreed, themselves, to begin such a venture is more than doubtful, but, since it had already been taken in hand by others, since Baxter and the Gilberts were names well enough known to many to command respect and affection, and since Coke—inspired by finding a plan for the establishment of missions among the heathen already in existence with glorious results—had described what he saw and hoped for with such eloquent, exultant self-abandon, the Conference gladly set down the new stations in the *Minutes*, and appointed Coke himself as their own representative in relation to the work in the West Indies.

Nothing could have pleased him better. His heart was full of the West Indies, and wherever he went he talked of Antigua and its people, of Columbus, of the French men-of-war and privateers, of the pirates that had ravaged their way to notoriety in the Caribbean waters, of the lovely hills and seas and islands, and, above all, of the slaves, many of them still in the condition of paganism and barbarity in which they had lived in the African bush villages.

Here, indeed, was something to plead for. His *Plan* for the missionary enterprise gained a new meaning. He had to find money to support something actual, not something remote and visionary. Wherever he went, he spoke of missions. Wherever he spoke, he made collections. Wherever he stayed, he pulled money from the pockets of his hosts. "I beg from door to door," he told his friends without shame. In 1789 he had so moved the Methodist people that the Conference formed the first "Missionary Committee"; though it seems quite certain that they had in their minds a group of men who would have the unhappy task of controlling Coke's begging and spending, rather than encouraging his appeals! Even Wesley himself, on occasion, told him that he was inconsiderate, injudicious and hasty, and would do his cause more harm than good by his indiscriminate money-raising.

Nothing would stop him, now. It was not as though he had seen once, and once only, and the memory would fade. He refreshed his acquaintance with the islands by stopping there on most of the trips he made to America between his providentially disastrous voyage in 1784, and 1802, when he paid his last visit.

Every visit brought him something to rejoice over, but each one gave him renewed anxiety and distress. Matters were not well in the West Indies, and the advent of Methodism made this clear.

About the time that Coke set off on his second visit, 1788, William Wilberforce, in conversation with Zachary Macaulay and the members of the Clapham Sect, was being forced to the conclusion that he must devote himself, his whole life if necessary, to the abolition of the slave-trade and the freeing of the slaves. Already Charles Wesley's school friend, Lord Mansfield, the Chief Justice of England, had declared that every man was free on British soil, and that any slave landing in England was thereby a freeman. The colonists in the West Indies looked askance at this judgment. They depended for their livelihood on slave-labour in the plantations, as well as for their comfort on slaves in the home. The great ports of Bristol and Liverpool, where the rings to which slaves were shackled still remain, were the home bases of ships engaged in the slave-trade. Many a great house there and in London was built, not on slave-labour, but on the proceeds of snatching negroes from their African homes, transporting them in indescribably filthy and congested quarters below the decks of slave-ships, and selling them to the planters at exorbitant rates of profit. The planters wanted workers, and anything which tended to make a slave discontented or rebellious was naturally strongly opposed.

Education was out of reach of the slaves; normal standards of living did not exist for them, so that they were encouraged to breed but not permitted to marry; leisure was denied them; the Church and clergy existed, apparently, solely for the consolation of the white people.

Methodism, with its genius for going to those who needed the gospel most, went to the slaves, taught them of the love of God, and made them aware of the value of their own souls. No wonder the planters were frightened that the slaves might in time come to place a new value on their bodies as well.

Coke, thrilled by his first visit, found much to encourage him on his second, but at the same time he noticed reasons for fearing the future.

His ship, commanded by a godly captain, gave him a very different reception and farewell from the blasphemous crew of his earlier vessel. When he left it at Barbados they wept and cheered as he went ashore. Here he found a group of people who were, apparently, waiting for the gospel. A number of Irish Methodist soldiers, part of the garrison of the island, supported by a local tradesman, formed his first congregation and took over and prepared a hall to act as a church for the missionary he left behind. The other two men whom he had brought this time he sent away the same day to St. Vincent, to save the heavy hotel charges.

Passing quickly amongst the other islands, he found John Baxter attempting to start a mission amongst the cannibal islanders, the Caribs, who now inhabited part of St. Vincent, and went on to Jamaica. On this voyage he began the mission in the south, and on his next, in 1790, he penetrated into Spanish Town and other places towards the north and north-west.

In Kingston he spoke easily to a full congregation on the first evening, but not without interruption on the second. He had hardly begun his sermon, having preached for about ten minutes, when the noise of a crowd of tipsy youths of fashion was heard on the stairs. Ready to make sport of the new parson, they pushed their way to the front of the crowd and began to shout and bang their swords.

"Who seconds this fellow?" they cried, in the duelling phrase of the day.

Up jumped a man from the front seats. "I second him, against men or devils," he answered. There was a stir in the congregation. The surprised young challenger waited for support. A lady of fashion rose, who had known John Wesley in London and been a member of the Society there. Without extravagance of phrase she began to denounce the interrupters, and when they finally slunk away down the stairs, having been warned against infamy, drunkenness, ungodliness and the fires of hell, they were a very much more sober and subdued group of mohocks.

Coke says calmly, in his account of the happening, "the congregation were so discomposed that I gave out another hymn, chose another text and preached to an eager and attentive audience" another sermon.

On his second visit to Jamaica, landing without friends, with only a recommendation to a gentleman who gave him an excellent dinner but no encouragement, he was forced to preach in a playhouse which had once been used as a church, and there once again, despite interruption, he founded a little Methodist society.

Before Coke preached in the playhouse, however, he had begun to understand that such interruptions were not casual and accidental. They were symptomatic of the attitude of the greater part of the white people of the islands towards Methodism, or any Church which stood by the negroes.

The first results of such hostility he discovered in the Dutch island of St. Eustatius, on his second visit.

On his arrival in the West Indies he had found the governor and his people polite, if not friendly, and the presentation of his credentials had appeared to satisfy them, so that they would allow him to preach and his Methodist negro congregation to continue in worship. This time there was a new situation. Governor Rennolds had turned on the leader of the Methodist slaves and had him flogged for his preaching. Black Harry had replied, with daring, "Christ was flogged; why should I not be?" He had been flogged harder for his blasphemy. Released, he had continued his work, and had finally been sold away from the island to an American slave-owner. Coke found him years later, a freeman, still bearing witness in America.

Rennolds then enacted what Coke described as one of the most barbarous laws since the Roman emperors first began to persecute the Church.

"If any white person should be found *praying* with his brethren—for the first offence he should be fined fifty pieces of eight; for the second, one hundred pieces; and, for the third, he should be whipped, his goods confiscated, and he should be banished from the island."

The second part was worse.

"If a coloured man be found *praying*—for the first offence he should receive thirty-nine lashes; and, for the second, if free, he should be whipped and banished; but if a slave, he should be whipped every time."

Coke put this down to the intolerance of the Dutch governor, a tyrant whose cruelty was notorious amongst the islanders, but when he returned, on his third visit in 1790, it was evident that the enmity to Methodism's work amongst the slaves was more widespread than he thought.

There was a new governor in St. Eustatius, Rennolds having been recalled. Coke visited him with hope, and was "received with great rudeness." The work on the neighbouring island of Saba, under the rule of the Dutch authorities, had been stopped and the missionary deported. Coke himself saw two negro women flogged for attending a prayer-meeting, and heard them proclaim their allegiance to Christ as the blood ran from their lacerated backs.

Even in Antigua, where relations were more friendly than anywhere else between white and black, John Baxter had been attacked by a crowd of ruffians, who had beaten him up and left him by the roadside.

In Jamaica, where on his first visit Coke had been supported against the rude interruptions of the roystering bucks of the town by the whole congregation, there were evident the first outcroppings of what was to become the most serious succession of persecutions in the islands. William Hammit's life had been threatened on more than one occasion, and he had been stoned in the street. The church which he had built—the largest in the islands—was attacked by a mob which was determined to pull it to pieces, and was prevented from setting it on fire only by the intervention of four magistrates who were forced, against their own desires, to intervene.

The local Press vilified the Methodists, and described Dr. Coke, to his astonishment, as a common horse-thief from England who had taken the disguise of a parson to help him in escaping to America.

Again, the minister was thrust into prison, and the magistrates sought to declare him and the Methodist preaching-place a public nuisance, within the meaning of the Act, so that they might be silenced and destroyed.

In St. Vincent a mob broke into the chapel, trampled books and furnishings, broke the furniture, and finally took the pulpit Bible and hung it in chains on the nearest gallows.

Matthew Lumb, in Tortola, was thrust into prison under an ordinance specifically aimed at silencing his preaching, and which imposed upon preachers who had no authority from the Government—they refused him such authority—a fine of £18 for the first offence, flogging and banishment for the second, and, for the third, if any man had the temerity to return, death. Lumb refused to acknowledge such an order and went on preaching to black and white alike. He was taken to prison and continued to preach through the bars of his cell. Here Coke found him and, though the majority of the islanders respected him and disliked the Act, which had been passed by a group of dissolute planters in the House of Assembly, neither he nor his friends could do anything to help. One wealthy man offered to pay Lumb's fine if he would desist from preaching and thus being thrust into prison again, but Lumb naturally refused.

Coke left him there in his cell and returned to London, his mind full of whippings, burnings, stonings, imprisonments and persecution. Something must be done. But what?

Fortunately for the West Indies, some of those men with whom Coke, in an earlier day at Oxford, had talked and probably gambled, were rising to positions of authority in the Government services. He remembered Lord Addington and Lord Liverpool, and wrote a careful letter to the Colonial Office, stating the case for religious freedom and tolerance, and showing what was happening to the Methodists of the West Indies.

There were occasions when it was a happy thing for Methodism in its early days that its acknowledged leaders were men of quality as well as character, and that people like John Wesley and Thomas Coke had access to those in high places. This was such a time.

Within a very short period the Colonial Secretary had sent to the West Indian islands, instituted inquiries about the character and behaviour of the Methodists, received favourable reports and issued orders for complete religious freedom for whites and slaves alike. These orders were not always obeyed, especially in Jamaica, but they made a great deal of difference to the lives of the West Indian Methodists, who were under Coke's supervision and for whom he was responsible to the Conference. The whole matter touched him at his heart. The islands were, it seemed to him, his own mission-field. Anything he could do for them, he would. He spent little time there, when all his visits are counted—probably it was not more than a year altogether—yet those visits and his constant interest were the foundation of all the present work in the West Indies, and the beginning of the missionary triumphs of the Methodist Church.

At the turn of the century, when Coke gave up his special responsibility for this work, the one missionary, John Baxter, had been replaced by twelve, and Baxter's fifteen hundred converts had risen to a membership of seven thousand.

CHAPTER SIX

SHIPWRECKS AND SLAVERY
(1787–1803)

"I RODE."

"I came."

"I went."

Day after day Francis Asbury made such entries in his diary. His journal is the restless itinerary of a man who was so hard driven by the urgency of his mission to preach the gospel and establish the Church all over America that he never had time to be still. To be ruled by such a man was, for the American preachers, to be constantly inspired to new endeavours and endless labour. To be his colleague, even his occasional colleague, as Coke was on his nine visits to America, was to accept hardship and danger, as well as encouragement.

Coke was not a man who sought honour for its own sake; he was too devoted to his ministry for that charge to hold any truth. He accepted it when it came, with some pride, but, although from the beginning he was honoured by preachers and people alike in America, he knew quite well whenever he set off on a fresh voyage across the Atlantic that he was undertaking a journey full of hazards, which would lead him into a period of weary travels, difficult enterprises and almost unavoidable danger.

Looking back, like the first great missionary, he could recount a lifetime of weariness, hunger, cold and danger, of peril from his own countrymen and from barbarians, of shipwreck, riot and almost certain death.

Why, then, did he continue, over a period of twenty years, to undertake eighteen journeys across the Atlantic?

He went to America first because John Wesley sent him to set up a new constitution for the Methodist Church there. He went again because he wished to report on what was happening there to the Methodist Conference in England. He continued to go, partly because he wanted to keep in touch with the Church he had seen growing, partly because it gave him an opportunity of "overseeing" the work in the first mission-field of Methodism, the West Indies, but most of all because the Methodist people and preachers in America persuaded him to do so. They valued his counsel, they enjoyed his preaching and, above all, they loved the man himself.

Nothing could prevent his trying to reach people whom he loved and who loved him. That was one of the most powerful impulses of all his missionary work in America, the West Indies, Africa or the East. He loved people. He loved them even more because he knew so much of the love of God in his own life, and he could not bear that others should be deprived of the knowledge of that saving love of God, in Christ, which meant all the world to him.

While the American preachers grew more and more to appreciate him, there was, in the beginning, a certain amount of suspicion and even hostility to one who, in culture, was so very different from the pioneering evangelists to whom they were accustomed, and who, in any case, represented the nation from which they had broken free. They loved and honoured Wesley, to whom they owed their spiritual lives, but they made it clear that he did not understand much of their new situation and that they would not be bound by his fiat from over the water. It was on this matter that Coke first found the preachers opposed to him.

On his second visit, in 1787, Wesley had found it "wise" to alter the date of the American Conference. The preachers were quite frank in their statement that they regarded this as a presumptuous interference with their rights and that, if Coke were to remain a fellow-labourer with them from time to time, he must come as the spiritual representative of the British Conference and not as the bearer of its commands. Francis Asbury was their chosen leader and, though he might make many decisions in consultation with Coke, they stood as the decisions of the Methodist Church in America.

The doctor had to walk a difficult path at times, assailed from both sides, and it is not surprising that he more than once lost his balance. Such an occasion occurred on his third visit, in 1788.

General Washington had been elected President of the United States. The Methodists, during the war, because of their British connections, had been suspected of disloyalty, and many of the preachers, including Asbury, with not a few of the rank-and-file members of the Church, had been persecuted or imprisoned. There was no longer any doubt of their position. Those who felt unable to live under the new constitution had withdrawn across the border to the British Colony of Canada, where they did remarkable pioneering service for the Church. Those who remained were true subjects of the free nation. It seemed appropriate to some of the preachers that this should be stated clearly and openly, and Asbury talked the matter over with Coke. Whoever first suggested the move, Coke was entirely in favour of what was proposed. Why should not an address to the President be drawn up and presented from the Methodist Church?

It was hardly thought of before it was done. It was not couched in the best of phrases, and the authors would have written better had they thought longer. It was not its beauty of language that caused the trouble, however, but its contents.

The President was urged to maintain "the preservation of those civil and religious liberties which have been transmitted to us by the Glorious Revolution."

The new constitution and republican system, from which kingship had been banished, was acknowledged "to be the admiration and pattern of the world."

To this document, advocating republicanism and glorying in the outcome of a war which had lost to Britain the greatest and oldest part of her colonial empire, Coke and Asbury set their hands and seals. Even the Americans were shocked at the foolish daring of a citizen of England, a subject of His Majesty King George III, signing the Address. Some were angry that Coke should meddle with an affair which obviously did not concern him.

The annoyed surprise of the Americans was nothing compared with the reception which awaited Coke when he returned to England and had to defend himself before the following Conference.

As usual, their anger was short-lived when they found the repentant doctor devoting himself to his preaching tours once more. Because he had to be in Britain for the Irish and English Conferences in June or July, his labours in America had, as a rule, to be undertaken during the winter. In the rigorous conditions he had to endure in the backwoods and the prairies he suffered greatly.

He followed Asbury's horse in the woods. The leader was racked with pain, as usual, but he led Coke forty-seven miles on one day and forty-four on the following one. Food was ham, with a little corn, day after day. Hospitality was willing, but meagre, and the preachers had often to lie on the floor, covered only by their riding blankets. Coke writes: "I am covered from top to toe in flannel, but still cold." Occasionally they saw the trails of the Red Indians, and more than once came across the marks of their raids and depredations—burned cottages, destroyed crops, now and then a scalped corpse. Flooded rivers and snowbound forests were natural barriers to the travelling preachers, but no weather made any difference.

"There is nothing out to-day but the crows and the Methodist preachers," ran a current proverb amongst the backwoods people.

It was not only the natural barriers which proved difficult to overcome, however, but the hostility of a section of the wealthy population. Neither Coke nor his friends ever wavered in their uncompromising gospel, and he notes, with truculent rejoicing, on one occasion— "My sermon gave huge offence to the unregenerate rich, praise God!"

Coke was thirty-seven when he first went to America to ordain Asbury. He did not cease his visits until he was fifty-six. If it had involved only the hazards of the pioneering preachers our respect for him would have been very high, but hardly a voyage passed without incident, and each must have made him disposed to vow that he would never go again.

French privateers were not idle at sea after the end of

the Revolution, and towards the end of his voyaging Britain was at war with France again on her own affairs. The French Revolution had degenerated into the "Terror," and Napoleon was threatening the insular safety of the "shopkeepers of Britain." In addition, there were the normal dangers of sea-going in sailing-ships which were seldom examined and often nearly unseaworthy.

On the second voyage out, which began with gales in the Channel and ended with their midnight anchorage at Antigua more than three months later, there had been the recurrent threat of capsizing in mid-Atlantic. On the fourth, when he was hoping to initiate a mission to the Red Indians, he was wrecked again on the American coast.

The visit of 1796 was disastrous from the beginning. The ship bore the name of *Friendship,* and no vessel could have been more inaptly named. As he did on every occasion, he paid his own fare—no expenses were ever charged to the Conference—and this time he paid an additional forty guineas for a friend. Everything was bad—accommodation, language, company and food. The captain was a drunken, blasphemous lout who hated religion and did all he could to make his passengers uncomfortable. After six weeks at sea, when it seemed that they must inevitably be wrecked either by bad weather or by bad seamanship, they almost ran down a hulk in mid-Atlantic. Most of the crew had been lost, and one woman, returning to England after many years in the West Indies, had been washed away after she had managed to cling for days to the wreckage. There were left only the captain, the mate, seven seamen and a woman with her small child. They had spent five days on the hulk drinking sea-water and eating leather from the covering of the hatch. Such were the perils of sailing-ships in the eighteenth century! It was with blasphemous reluctance that the captain of the *Friendship* took them on board.

Much later than he intended, too late already, it seemed, to get to the important Conference at Baltimore, they anchored in Chesapeake Bay. The captain refused to let Coke go ashore with his baggage in the pilot boat. He was told he might go himself and leave his baggage, but the doctor had done that once before and knew what happened to his luggage. When he at last decided to take the risk it was too late. The pilot boat was gone. He then offered to give the captain the fare for the pilot boat and go himself in a fishing-boat nearby, and this curious financial offer the captain accepted, allowing Coke's French friend to remain behind with the luggage and see it ashore at the end of the voyage. He landed with one clean shirt in his greatcoat pocket—his only possessions to take him to the Conference. The sloop which was to convey him, and for which he had paid, after getting ashore, was unable to sail, and at last he managed to persuade a friendly senator to lend him a horse and send him on his way.

At this Conference, after Coke had visited America six times with growing appreciation from the Church there, he was pressed graciously but urgently to forgo his connection with British Methodism and transfer his ministry permanently to America. With customary impetuosity, deeply moved by the friendship which found expression in this way, and hardly recovered from the attitude of hostility he had met at home, Coke agreed to join the Methodist Episcopal Church of America and subject himself to the authority of Francis Asbury, its head.

One thing he had forgotten was the missionary enterprise which he had been advocating in Britain for ten years. In the end he did not transfer his ministry. It was wise that he remained a member of the British Conference. America was less able, and would perhaps at this stage have been even less willing, than Britain to dislocate its work at home for what was still a vague possibility of success in the East.

On his next voyage, the following year, when on the *President* he had a far kinder and more genial captain than that of the *Friendship,* a worse disaster overtook them. They began by seeing sharks and running into storms, but were given warning of something more dangerous than either by a Danish vessel which they passed. Hardly had they left this ship when they sighted the French privateer of which they had been told. They had not enough speed of sail to escape, and were boarded and captured by the Frenchman. The schooner took over the officers and several of the crew, and ordered the captain to sail for the Spanish colony of Porto Rico, where that Government at once declared ship and cargo a prize for the French and made the captain and his crew prisoners. Of Coke they took little notice, apart from commandeering his baggage. He seemed to them an innocent little priest who might roam the world without doing harm to anyone, and he was sent about his business, courteously enough, by his French and Spanish captors and allowed to make his way to America. Once more, as on his previous disastrous voyage, he was left with a few papers and less clothes.

In 1803, with Britain blockaded around all her coasts, the French and British fleets playing hide-and-seek amongst the ports of Spain and Bay of Biscay, and Nelson and the French admirals criss-crossing in the

Atlantic waters between Gibraltar and the West Indies, Coke sailed once more into deliberate danger, which he escaped on the way out but not so completely on the way home. A French man-of-war sighted them and, giving chase, bore down on them rapidly for twenty-four hours, only giving up the pursuit when British ships of the line appeared over the horizon. On an earlier voyage it had been Hood's fleet which dislodged a pursuer in almost the same place.

Thus, time after time, the little doctor welcomed any danger so long as he might exercise his world ministry. Riding a hundred miles a week with the preachers through swamps and morasses where the water was above their knees, and being turned adrift by evil-minded skippers or chased by enemy gun-boats, once or twice would have been quite sufficient for most men. Not even Wesley himself, with all his courageous facing of riotous miners or mobs in the new industrial towns, was called on to show such calm courage or resolute endurance. With all this, Coke set himself to make more virulent enemies in America.

No man with a heart so capable of pity as his could for long endure to see the sufferings of the slaves without protesting. William Wilberforce, who stood as an independent member of Parliament and devoted the whole of his career and fortune to the cause of freedom for the slaves, received the last letter which Wesley ever wrote, a brief note commending his courage and urging him to go on with his work. Wilberforce in turn wrote to Coke, who put his cause to the British Conference. What he was willing to say about the evils of trafficking in negroes, wrenched from their homes, in the security of a Conference chapel, he was equally ready to say in the slave-owning communities of America.

He presented, on behalf of the Methodist Church there, a petition to George Washington urging him to undertake the cause of the slaves and set up laws giving them their freedom.

There was no doubt about the Methodist attitude in America, from the outset, towards those who held slaves. In one of its earliest Conferences it set out the question in its *Minutes*: "Does this Conference acknowledge that slavery is contrary to the laws of God, man and nature; hurtful to society, and contrary to the dictates of conscience and religion; and doing that which we would not that others should do to us and ours?" Those who held slaves were to be disciplined. Preachers who kept slaves were to set them free or themselves to be discharged from their office. The decisions of the Church were in complete accordance with the original attitude of the colonists who had opposed slavery, but who had been compelled by the British Government to accept the system.

For many reasons the policy of the Conference had to be modified, but its preachers denounced the system, its worthier sons freed their slaves and Coke joined in the campaign of humanity whenever he was in the country.

He was stoned for his trouble, and had to be silent, as a consequence, where he would often have liked to preach.

One fashionable lady cried out: "I will give fifty pounds to any man who will seize that little doctor and give him a hundred lashes." There were plenty of ruffians waiting to see the fun who responded to her call, and no doubt Coke would have been beaten very nearly to death if it had not been for the interference of a magistrate and an army officer standing by. As a consequence, Coke was worse hated in that area, but the magistrate who had stood by his side almost immediately freed his fifteen slaves, and some of his friends soon followed his example.

A typical entry in the *Journal* speaks of a funeral sermon which the doctor preached on a local magnate who upheld slavery. "I said nothing good of him, for he was a violent friend of slavery; and his interests in these parts being great amongst the Methodists he would have been a dreadful thorn in our side, if the Lord had not, in His mercy, taken him away!"

To incur the hot anger of the selfish and wealthy was no deterrent to such a lover of mankind. Until his last visit in 1803 he preached the same gospel of grace, with its attendant demands on the behaviour of Christian people towards their fellow-men. As a result, he was as honoured amongst the mass of the people in America as he was loved by the slaves and the generous-hearted islanders of the West Indies.

His position in Britain during this time was not so easy.

CHAPTER SEVEN

UNPOPULAR HERO
(1789-1799)

IN the spring of 1791 Coke was in America, at Philadelphia. He went home to supper with a merchant of Port Royal, and his host on the way gave him the news. Coke did not believe the rumour, until he was given a newspaper in the house. There could be no doubt of it.

John Wesley had died on the 2nd of March.

He was an old man, more than eighty years of age. His life had spanned nearly a whole century. He had lived in the reigns of Queen Anne and three of the Georges. He had known the long peace under the first Prime Minister, Walpole, and the "war of Jenkins' ear" which had broken it. He had seen Britain's empire spread into Canada and India in the middle of the century, and suffer the loss of the great American Colonies a few years later. He had witnessed the slow, certain transformation of much of England's countryside from agriculture to industry, with the resulting degradation of the men, women and children who trekked from the villages into the new towns. He had helped to set the four kingdoms on fire with a new spiritual zeal, and built up, under his own leadership, a society of people called Methodists who were to be found in strength in Britain, America and the West Indies, and to some extent all over the world in the military forces of the Crown.

Now, at last, the Methodist Church—it was no longer possible to think of it, after Wesley's many innovations, either as a mere "society" or as part of the Church of England—was without a leader.

Coke determined to hurry home.

The voyage cannot have been peaceful. He was aching to be in England, and deeply regretting that he had not been there to say farewell to the man who had brought him into Methodism and commissioned him to go out into all the world and preach the gospel to men. He was also wondering what place he would have in the new situation, and trying to surmise what difference his absence from England at the moment of Wesley's death might have made.

When the ship drew near the Cornish coast the look-out sighted a Cornish fishing-smack. Willing to shorten the journey by even a few hours, whatever it cost, Coke was lowered from the sailing-ship into the fishing-boat and agreed with the men to take him to land for three guineas. He was in London before the larger vessel had made port.

There are surprisingly few letters, in the voluminous correspondence that remains of Wesley's writings, between Wesley and Coke. It would have been valuable to have had more, but from the journals and the letters that we have it is clear that the relations of the two great men had not been so easy in Wesley's later years as they were in the beginning.

Wesley, with typical forthrightness, had once written: "Dr. Coke and I are like the French and the Dutch; the French have been compared to a flea and the Dutch to a louse. I creep like a louse, and the ground I get I keep; but the doctor leaps like a flea and is sometimes obliged to leap back again."

They valued each other highly; probably they loved each other; but differences in temperament strained their understanding as each grew more set in his ways and more convinced of his rightness.

Coke found Wesley lacking in world-vision. He deprecated the old man's sane and impartial summing up of a situation, when it prevented a leap in the dark, even a leap of faith. But on the whole he was more loyal to his leader than the old man was just to his helper.

Wesley disliked hastiness and impetuosity, and both these qualities were very evident in Coke at this period. Worse than this, he believed he saw in the aristocratic doctor an ambition which he wholeheartedly abhorred. In the very early days of their friendship he warned him of "the desire for applause." Coke's actions in America —especially his founding of a College bearing his own and Asbury's names and, more, his appropriation of the title "bishop"—seemed to confirm him in his judgment. "I am afraid both you and the doctor differ from me," he wrote to Asbury when he first heard of their new title. "I study to be little; you study to be great. I creep; you strut along."

Wesley's criticisms were harsher than they need have been, and to that extent they were unjust. At the same time they were largely shared by the preachers throughout Britain. Even if this had not been the case, however, it is quite certain that Coke would never have succeeded to the position of dictatorship which Wesley had occupied during the past fifty years. Methodism's affection for John Wesley was profound; anything which touched his honour touched the Church. But this did not mean that the preachers and people did not sometimes chafe under his commands, and what they accepted, now and then with reluctance, from a beloved leader they had no intention of inviting from anyone else.

It may have been Wesley's desire that Coke should, *in some sense,* be his successor. Coke was one of the three clergymen of the Established Church left within Methodism, and he would have continued much of the founder's policy. A second man whom Wesley favoured was Alexander Mather. The Conference knew of Wesley's preferences, but they made their own choice.

Hardly had Wesley been buried when William Thompson, stationed at Halifax, called a meeting of seven other influential preachers and, with them, issued a pamphlet which was given wide publicity throughout Methodism. It declared that there should never be "another king in Israel," and that, instead of having one acknowledged "overseer," the Conference should annually elect a President and a Secretary. To this plan Methodism very readily agreed.

Coke may reasonably have hoped that the Conference would do him the honour of making him its first President. Instead, he found an attitude of coldness and sometimes hostility which was evident wherever he went. What was the reason for this mistrust of one who had braved more dangers than any man in Methodism, had established missions throughout the West Indies, was held in high honour in America and was the only preacher other than the Wesleys known widely outside of Methodism?

British Methodism had not forgotten his action four years previously when he set his signature to the Address to the President of the United States, and thereby intimated his dissatisfaction with his own country and his possible disloyalty to the Crown.

Nor had it forgotten things that touched it more closely.

Coke's rise to authority had been amazingly swift, and in his flight upwards he had passed by many preachers who had been the servants of Methodism before he entered it. Some of them still recalled the part that he had had in framing the Deed of Declaration, and were inclined to blame him for their exclusion from the governing body of the Conference, the "Legal Hundred." Others were suspicious of his aristocratic background, his easy mixing with people not normally friendly with Methodists, and what they regarded as his jaunty bearing. Such attitudes may have been unchristian, but they were not unnatural.

Antipathy arose in general from more sincere causes. There was an honest opposition to missionary work being undertaken at that time. Coke's persistent begging for funds for work in the East appeared to be diverting money from causes which were nearer at hand and in more desperate need. Dreams of a Church rising up in the East were believed to be chimerical, and few men shared with him an ear so keenly attuned to the cries of need that they heard India or Africa calling out for the gospel. They dubbed him an "enthusiast," and put into the word all the venom and scorn which their opponents used when they spoke of the fanatical Methodists themselves. More than this, and more detrimental to the future of Methodism in Britain, they felt, was the fact that Coke was the leader of the "High Church" party within Methodism. This group—which desired the continuance of the liturgy and other church services, deprecated the administration of the sacraments by the majority of the preachers and advocated a continued loyalty to the Established Church—included some of the greatest amongst the preachers, but it had no whole-hearted following in a society which had grown up largely outside the Church and been repudiated by clergy and laymen alike.

Coke made several attempts to bring Methodism into line, if not into full reunion, with the Established Church. He attempted to unite the Methodist and the historical episcopal churches in America. He tried to persuade the Methodists in Britain to accept the principle of episcopacy and elect "bishops" amongst themselves. He gathered a group of selected preachers together with a view to asking a friendly Anglican, the Bishop of Lichfield, to ordain them as clergy of the Established Church and yet give them a roving commission to continue as they had been doing, preaching up and down the land wherever they would.

In all these things is to be traced that sudden response to an idea of the moment, involving action without reflection, which characterised the man throughout his life, and which accounted for many of his failures as well as much of his success.

The mind of Conference was clear when it met after Wesley's death. It wished Coke to be equally clear. It disliked his missionary advocacy, it distrusted his churchmanship, it feared his ambition and it was rightly suspicious of his impulsive judgments.

His friends tried to persuade him not to attend the Irish Conference. He insisted on going—and was rebuffed. For the first time since Wesley had sent him as his representative he was kept out of the Presidential chair.

He realised that it was unlikely that he would be elected to the same honour in Britain, and he was right. He was given the secondary honour of Secretary (his legal talents were too obvious for any other choice to be made), and William Thompson, the writer of the pamphlet which rejected autocracy, was chosen as first President.

For a year the whole of the missionary appointments —the stations in the West Indies—were dropped from the Conference list.

He was censured for his action in ordaining a preacher in France, and made to feel that he must act as the Conference wished and not as he might himself think best.

His disappointment, even distress, must have been severe at the attitude of his colleagues, and it was not eased by two failures in missionary advocacy.

The West Indies Methodists were still enduring great persecution when he managed to obtain an order from the King in Council granting religious toleration in the British islands. This success encouraged him to attempt to gain the same freedom for the Methodists in St. Eustatius and Saba, where Governor Rennolds, who had been reappointed to the islands, was perpetrating more savage cruelties than before. Taking a letter of commendation from some of his Government acquaintances, he went to Holland to plead the cause of the negroes. He was received with coldness and dismissed with something approaching rudeness. The Dutch had not forgotten what had happened to their prosperous islands at the hands of the British fleet, and were not disposed to grant requests to an itinerant clergyman whom they regarded as a stirrer-up of trouble and disaffection amongst their people. The persecution continued, despite the fact that the Governor's daughter in St. Eustatius became a class-leader amongst the despised Methodists.

A similar rebuff came to him in France.

There was little discrimination in Coke's choice of missionary methods. What came to hand must be used. When an appeal came to the Countess of Huntingdon for workers to go to France and set up a church in Paris, he offered to go himself and make arrangements on the spot. France was in the hands of the revolutionaries. Reason had been set on the throne of religion. Britain was becoming the worst-hated nation in Europe. The position of Britishers was insecure, and clerics were the objects of malicious mob-violence. Knowing all these things, Coke sailed for France in 1792.

At first things did not go too badly. He chose to travel with a French merchant returning home, and they went by way of the Channel Islands, where he picked up a preacher named de Quetville and ordained him. Together they hired a sloop to take them to Grandville, in Normandy, and from there walked to Coutances, where they stayed as the guests of a sick nobleman. At Conseule, not far away, was stationed a French-speaking Methodist preacher, Mahé. He, too, Coke ordained and took him with them. They travelled by *diligence* to Paris, the city of revolution, terror and death, where the *guillotine* had clacked up and down, slicing off the heads of noble and ignoble alike, and where priests and aristocrats had been torn to pieces by the maddened crowds.

At once things began to go wrong. The news had arrived of the death of the Countess of Huntingdon, the sponsor of the scheme to evangelise the ungodly of Paris. The letter-writers were discovered to be two impecunious teachers, completely useless either as workers or guarantors. Coke determined to risk more of his own money and hired a large hall, advertising his service widely. Six people came to worship, including the two teachers. He had arranged to purchase the hall and leave one of his two preachers in charge. When he came out of the "church" he discovered a crowd gathered outside.

There was no doubt about their attitude or about their intentions. A man was swinging a knotted rope in his hand. The spokesman, in the red cap of the revolutionaries, told him that if he did not promise to leave immediately he would be strung up to a lamp-post to kick his heels in a death agony as most of their own clergy had done. The mob was well practised. Coke looked round and saw a lamp-post all too conveniently near.

The next day he managed to have cancelled the deed by which he had hired the hall. With Mahé and de Quetville he left Paris and returned home.

Rebuked and rebuffed by Methodism in Britain, threatened in France, unsuccessful in Holland, with his missionary work discounted and his money-raising for it hampered by a committee, Coke was desperately unhappy, when he was not too busy to think of what had happened. For four years the position was the same, though the West Indian stations were retained on the *Minutes* and he was re-elected President of the Irish Conference.

In 1796 he decided to transfer his frustrated ministry to the Methodist Church in America.

Whether this act roused British Methodism to think more clearly of what it owed to him, we do not know. Perhaps the turmoil following Wesley's death was beginning to calm down and a new period was beginning in which the value of his services to the Church would have been seen more clearly. At any rate, the British

Conference in 1796 pleaded with him to change his mind, and deeply moved by their appeals he asked the Conference in America to revoke its decision accepting him as a member of the Methodist Church there.

Thenceforward there was a change of attitude. His missionary plans did not gain immediate acceptance— they were, indeed, frustrated for the next fifteen years —but there was a growing acceptance of the fact that *sometime* Methodism must discharge its wider responsibilities, and meanwhile the Conference was prepared to follow his lead in less tremendous issues and sanction missionary schemes for work which they could understand and see. His place became more secure as his ambition grew apparently less.

In 1797, the year in which Methodism set forth resolutions which meant its final severance from the Established Church, the Conference confirmed its affection for Coke by electing him President.

A P L A N

S O C I E T Y

Eſtabliſhment of Miſſions among the Heathens.

I. EVERY Perſon who fubſcribes Two Guineas yearly, or more, is to be admitted a Member of the Society.

II. A General Meeting of the Subſcribers ſhall be held annually, on the laſt Tueſday in January.

III. The firſt General Meeting ſhall be held on the laſt Tueſday in January, 1784, at No. 11, in Weſt-ſtreet, near the Seven Dials, London, at Three o'Clock in the Afternoon.

IV. At every General Meeting a Committee of Seven, or more, ſhall be choſen by the Majority of the Subſcribers, to tranſaƈt the Buſineſs of the Society for the enſuing Year.

V. The General Meeting ſhall receive and examine the Accounts of the Committee for the pre-ceding Year, of all Sums paid to the Uſe of the Society, of the Purpoſes to which the Whole, or any Part thereof, ſhall have been applied, and alſo the Report of all they have done, and the Advices they have received.

VI. The Committee, or the Majority of them, ſhall have Power, Firſt, To call in the Sums fubſcribed, or any Part thereof, and to receive all Colleƈtions, Legacies, or other voluntary Contributions. Secondly, To agree with any they ſhall approve, who may offer to go abroad, either as Miſſionaries, or in any Civil Employment. Thirdly, To procure the beſt Inſtruƈtion which can be obtained for ſuch Perſons, in the Language of the Country for which they are intended, before they go abroad. Fourthly, to provide for their Expences, in going and continuing abroad, and for their return Home, after ſuch Time, and under ſuch Circumſtances, as may be thought meſt expedient. Fifthly, To print the Scriptures, or ſo much thereof, as the Funds of the Society may admit, for the Uſe of any Heathen Country. And, Sixthly, to do every other Aƈt which to them may appear neceſſary, ſo far as the common Stock of the Society will allow, for carrying the Deſign of the Society into Execution.

VII. The Committee ſhall keep an Account of the Subſcribers Names, and all Sums received for the Uſe of the Society, together with ſuch Extraƈts of the Entries of their Proceedings and Advices, as may ſhew thoſe who are concerned, all that has been done both at Home and Abroad: which State ſhall be ſigned by at leaſt Three of the Committee.

VIII. The Committee for the New Year ſhall ſend a Copy of the Report for the paſt Year, to all the Members of the Society who were not preſent at the preceding General Meeting, and (free of Poſtage) to every Clergyman, Miniſter, or other Perſon, from whom any Colleƈtion, Legacy, or other Benefaƈtion, ſhall have been received, within the Time concerning which the Report is made.

IX. The Committee, if they ſee it neceſſary, ſhall have Power to chooſe a Secretary.

X. The Committee ſhall at no Time have any Claim on the Members of the Society, for any Sum which may exceed the common Stock of the Society.

N. B. Thoſe who ſubſcribe before the firſt General Meeting, and to whom it may not be con-venient to attend, are deſired to favour the General Meeting by Letter (according to the above Direƈtion) with any important Remarks which may occur to them on the Buſineſs, that the Sub-ſcribers preſent may be aſſiſted as far as poſſible, in ſettling the Rules of the Society to the Satis-faƈtion of all concerned.

CHAPTER EIGHT

THE TRAVELLER AT HOME
(1798–1811)

IT has been suggested that if John Wesley had had a better wife he might have stayed more often at home and Methodism would have suffered by his domestic happiness. Coke was not subjected to this temptation. He had no home. His parents had died by the time he was established within Methodism and, until he was almost sixty, he had never married. There is no doubt that, had he done so, his affectionate nature would have been constantly torn between the love of home and children and the love of the world outside. Free of any natural ties, he had been able to travel as no man in Methodism had done, and to devote his love to his spiritual children in Britain and the West.

At the turn of the century he was still riding up and down the country, preaching his missionary gospel and pleading for funds. Wherever he went he tried to gather names of possible subscribers from his hosts and preachers whom he met.

In 1805 he rode into Bristol. Talking with William Pawson, the preacher there, he asked him if he knew of any possible donors. There ought to be some, he thought, for Bristol, like Bath nearby, had a noted spa at Hot Wells, where the wealthy and sick came to take the waters. John Wesley himself, he recalled, had come here in his middle age when he believed himself threatened by death from consumption.

"There is a lady now staying at Hot Wells," said Pawson, "who, I should not wonder, would give you something handsome. If you like, I will show you myself where she is lodging."

Together they went through Clifton and down into the Wells. Pawson introduced him to Miss Penelope Goulding Smith who, he had previously pointed out, was the heiress of a large fortune and a good Christian woman of wide sympathies. Coke pleaded the cause of the West Indian slaves with passion, but even he was surprised when, at the end of the interview, she told him to come to her house in Wiltshire and she would give him a hundred guineas.

A little later he came through the soft Wiltshire countryside to the little town of Bradford, on the Avon. He discovered, to his delight, that the lady had determined to double her subscription. She seemed willing to give even more, and anxious to hear of the work he was doing. Friendship grew out of the gift. In April 1805, at the age of fifty-eight, Coke was married.

His domestic life was short. Five years later, Mrs. Coke died.

Strangely enough, after so long a life of celibacy, he married a Liverpool lady, Miss Ann Loxdale, a year after his first wife's death. They had hardly been married a year before she, too, was dead. Coke was an old man when she died in 1812—far older, in some ways, than his sixty-five years—burned out by passion and exhausted by constant travel and physical hardship.

During the years of his marriage, and just before them, he had been engaged on work nearer home, and his friends in British Methodism saw close at hand the results of his inspiration and directing energy. In the twelve years between 1799 and 1811 he had put his hand to many things, none of them unimportant.

Children had become more and more neglected, and thus more undisciplined and unhealthy, during the middle part of the century, when they were being forced to work long hours for little money in mines, factories, mills and chimneys. Robert Raikes and Hannah Ball were pioneers in gathering these children together on Sundays for spiritual and elementary education. Coke, with his eye on the Far West and the farther East, had apparently little time to spare for such activities, but he knew what was happening and encouraged the Methodist people to take their share in the work. When he began to spend more time in Britain he took up the cause of the children, advocating Sunday Schools wherever he preached. In Cornwall, at any rate, he was one of the pioneers of the movement, and there is evidence that in the centre of the county he was the first man to start them.

Men and women who suffered in any way always found a place in his heart, and the Napoleonic wars brought plenty of suffering in their train. Many families who had received news of sailor sons and husbands being killed or drowned at Trafalgar, St. Vincent, the Nile or the attempt to break through Napoleon's blockade, were not sorry to see ten great hulks in the Medway crowded with French prisoners of war, many of them sailors. They lived in filthy conditions, were not allowed off the ships and had nothing to give them interest or hope. Visitors were seldom admitted, and there were no chaplains on the ships.

William Toaze, the preacher stationed at Sevenoaks, had been at work in the Channel Islands and Normandy. He spoke French fluently and understood the French people. While most of the British people were aware only of Napoleon striding about Europe and threatening to eat up the rest of the world, and thought of the French as bloody and ruthless soldiers who flocked after him and did his merciless bidding, Toaze knew how many in France were alienated by Napoleon's ruthlessness and how they, too, had suffered through the long-drawn-out years of war. He visited the ships and preached on the quarter-deck, finding a pathetic welcome amongst the ragged prisoners. They asked him to come again. When he made the attempt he was informed that the commissary for the ships regarded his work as an interference and had forbidden him to board the hulks.

Toaze appealed to Coke. Again the doctor's acquaintance with those in high places proved its value. It was nearly fifty years since he had been at Oxford with Lord Liverpool, but the Earl very readily repealed the commissary's ban, and for the four years before Waterloo the prisoners had services, schools and friendship in their dreary river prisons, as well as in other camps throughout the south country where they were incarcerated. The work of the Protestant Church in France gained not a little because of the memories they took back with them of Methodist people and their kindness.

Methodism throughout the world has always owed much to military and naval men. Baxter was a Government servant in the naval dockyards, and the West Indian missions bear him a great debt. More than a quarter of Wesley's early preachers had fought at Fontenoy and Dettingen and other Continental battle-fields. India, China, South Africa and Australasia had the Methodist fervour and gospel taken to them by soldiers, and in American Methodism one of the greatest and most fascinating figures of the pioneering days was Captain Thomas Webb. Coke had known Webb and his comrades in the army, and valued the work they were doing. More than once he heard from men stationed in the East of the need for missionaries, and of their own attempts to preach to Indians and Ceylonese. His zeal was stirred again and again in this way.

It is not surprising, then, that when an appeal came from a group of soldiers stationed at Gibraltar he was ready to respond to it. He knew that an earlier group of soldiers there had been posted ten years before to the East, and that one of them, Andrew Armour, had done tremendously valuable work in Madras and was continuing it in Ceylon. Now others, in the fever-stricken base on the Rock, asked for a chaplain. His requests to the Conference caused them to send a preacher, with his wife and child. The immediate result was tragedy, for the missionary died of yellow fever almost as soon as he arrived. He was replaced by another, however, and the chaplains to the garrison did most useful service amongst the soldiers and in preparing the way for a later mission to the Roman Catholics on the Spanish mainland.

Methodism in Britain was organised in a system of circuits to which preachers were appointed who had to oversee the work, superintend the classes and bands, administer discipline and preach constantly. They were, on the whole, good men, and devoted to their work. Not all were highly educated, though it is surprising that there were so few ill-educated amongst them. Most of them found the work to which they were appointed as much as they were able to do, and more. It was unthinkable that many should have the opportunity to break into new areas and begin fresh ventures, yet there were large tracts of England, as well as Wales and Ireland, where neither Wesley nor his helpers had found a hearing.

Devonshire, parts of East Anglia and the neighbouring midlands, Kent and the agricultural counties of central England had witnessed no mighty revivals of religion, and had been largely neglected by the Conference since Wesley's death. The claims of the ordinary work, and the drain on resources necessitated by Coke's own demands for the West Indies and elsewhere, were sufficient to intimidate the Conference from initiating yet more undertakings which might have poor results.

Ireland, Coke knew well from his annual visits, was largely ignorant, neglected and superstitious. Methodism had never entered some parts of the country. He resolved to begin a new type of work—the sending of missionaries to those at home in addition to the heathen overseas. The scheme caught the imagination of many people. Here, at any rate, was something they could see and the results of which they could measure with reasonable accuracy. Gideon Ouseley was sent into the Irish countryside, with a group of fellow-preachers, to proclaim the gospel to those who had never heard it spoken with the Methodist accent. It was stated in the *Minutes of Conference* that Brother Ouseley was "at liberty to follow the Providence of God."

Providence led him to great success, and to more than a little trouble. In Roman Catholic parishes he was assaulted and driven out, yet the people listened in spite of the fact that their priests stood over them, threatened them with penance and excommunication, and horse-whipped them back through the streets to their homes.

Coke was able to gain protection for the preachers throughout the rebellions of these years, and on more than one occasion military officers granted them access to the barracks of British troops or hemmed in the evangelists with artillerymen or squadrons of cavalry who listened with great respect and, often, with new conviction.

Ireland had great reason to be thankful for the work of Ouseley and his fellows.

Wales presented a different problem. In the south, Methodism of a Calvinist type had maintained its stronghold. Before Coke left Brecon for the University there were many who found in Wesley's and Whitefield's preaching the thing they were seeking. Yet in the north and in the more remote and mountainous parts of the country were hundreds, thousands, of people who had never had the gospel preached to them in their own tongue. Nor had the Scriptures been translated into Welsh.

In 1800, the year after Irish Home Missions were begun, a Welsh layman, Edward Jones, began preaching to his countrymen in their own tongue. So great was his success that he appealed to Coke for men who would support him. The Conference of 1801 had already finished its work and passed its final list of preachers' stations when Coke returned from America, though it was still in session. It had not finally dispersed when he came in and began to speak. Here he was pleading, not for those far away, but for his own Welsh people. Before the preachers left they had reconsidered the stationing for the coming year and appointed half a dozen men to work in Wales, with the same sort of roving commission as those in Ireland.

The mission continued until Coke's death, when, like

other things that had depended on his eloquent advocacy, it was suspended.

Ireland and Wales led on to England. Were there not tracts of their own homeland where such men were needed, people began to ask, and Coke was again the first to urge Conference to respond to the need that they had just begun to recognise. First, eight men were appointed to work in the neglected villages of Rutland, in Thetford, Devizes, Collumpton, Taunton, Ulverstone, and Meols. To these areas were added, the next year, others in Lincolnshire, Worcestershire, Herefordshire, Suffolk, Essex, Surrey and Devon. English Home Missions had begun.

Coke was no mere advocate of lost or far-away causes. He took to his heart impulsively anything or anyone needing help. He gave himself and committed others to undertakings large and small, wise and foolish. During the first decade of the nineteenth century, French prisoners, neglected children, soldiers on active service, Irish and Welsh peasants who spoke only their own mother-tongues, and English villages all over the land, had reason to be grateful for his enterprise, his sympathy and evangelical love of all mankind. These labours, together with two visits to America, not a little literary work, the devotion to his new home and constant preaching tours would seem to have been sufficient to exhaust any normal man.

Yet it was during these years that his most effective advocacy of missions overseas was heard, and he at last began to persuade the Methodist people of their responsibility towards the East.

CHAPTER NINE

THAT THE WORLD MIGHT KNOW
(1790–1812)

THE first Missionary Committee of the Methodist Church in Great Britain appeared on the *Minutes of Conference* in 1790.

Four years previously, Coke and his companions had been driven into the island harbour of Antigua. Missionary work there had been strengthened and new stations begun in other West Indian islands. Back in England, between his visits, Coke had begged money for the support of the work and tried to extend it when he revisited the islands with new missionaries. He had no concern with denominational boundaries. It was the work of God, and the people of God must support it. He begged where he could, and took subscriptions from Methodists, Baptists and members of the Established Church without distinction. In the years that followed he continued this haphazard method, augmenting the money he received by taking collections, whenever he was allowed, in the Methodist societies where he preached up and down the country.

Many of the preachers and trustees were unhappy about his appeals, and Wesley, as we have seen, urged him to be more discriminating. To effect some sort of control over so unorthodox a man, Conference appointed a Committee of Preachers who should examine books and ledgers, and generally try to restrain the wilder schemes which he could undoubtedly be expected to put forward. Coke's relationship to the Committee was vague and it apparently did very little actual work, though the doctor later fulminated against having to waste nearly every Friday morning, when he might have been begging yet more money, accounting for what he had already raised and spent to a group of preachers who wished, he felt, to rein in his enthusiasm. His impulsiveness was no doubt to be seen in his keeping of his accounts, where sums collected from outside, the proceeds of collections, his own giving to make up deficiencies and his wife's unending contributions were all mixed up.

There was no suspicion of his use of the money. Everyone knew he very often gave more from his own purse than he raised from outside, and they had no hesitation about appointing him the agent of the Society. Contributions from overseas, account-books and statements were to be sent direct from superintendents in the overseas stations to him, and he alone had the actual disbursement of what was raised. Not even in the years of his overshadowed reputation was there any question of his right to represent Methodism and the West Indian stations to each other.

By 1804, however, the financial affairs were in such a tangle, mixed up as they were with the accounts of the publishing house, that a new Committee of Finance and Advice was appointed to put them into some kind of order. This was done while Coke was away in America, and he took umbrage at the fact that anyone had interfered with work which he regarded as particularly his own. No dark mood lasted for long, however, and he was soon on the best of terms with those who were appointed to "help" him.

This interest in financial matters is not to be interpreted as a sign of conversion in the Conference to the missionary cause. Most of the preachers felt the time was inopportune, in spite of the fact that by the turn of the century William Carey and his colleagues had been in Bengal for some time, and others had grave doubts of the possibility of such work succeeding at all.

The work in the West Indies was going forward, it is true, but the Conference had been committed to that in a moment of high enthusiasm following on Coke's report, and it would not turn back. It cannot be doubted, on the other hand, that if the Conference, and not Coke, had had the responsibility of raising the money for the support of the work, it would have been much less inclined to carry it on in its present strength.

In addition, it should be remembered, the Conference was not called upon to bear the expense of most of Coke's journeys to and from the West Indies and America. He went as the representative of British Methodism, but he paid for his own passages, and sometimes those of the missionaries. He also bore not a little of the actual expenses of plant in the islands themselves.

The work in the West Indies, in spite of persecution in many islands, went forward wherever it had been established, and the missionaries and their island helpers constantly carried it farther afield.

On his last visit to the Caribbean area, Coke found that, instead of one preacher, Baxter, having the care of two thousand people, there were now ten preachers and a membership of seven thousand.

Before Coke's death Methodism had been established in ten of the most important islands, as well as other smaller ones. It had penetrated to Robinson Crusoe's island of Tobago, to the Bahamas and Bermuda, and from there to the mainland of British Guiana, where

Raleigh had lured his sailors with the fruitless quest of El Dorado. Coloured people had begun to preach, as pioneer evangelists, suffering great distress as a result. Demerara had become a base for the Church, though it was for a while given up when the preachers were deported, and those who were not allowed to stay had laid the foundations of the Church in Trinidad, the "land of the humming-bird."

Before he left the English shore for the last time, Coke knew that the seven thousand members and ten preachers of a few years earlier had been increased to seventeen thousand, with thirty missionaries, two of them coloured men and others island-born.

There could be no hesitation in regarding the work in the West Indies as the work of God.

Other projects, to which Methodism reluctantly agreed, were not so successful. The great example of failure was Sierra Leone.

This part of West Africa had been discovered by Portuguese navigators, who were followed by the first slave-traders from that country. Dutch and British slavers came not long afterwards. The decision of Lord Mansfield, freeing all slaves on British territories, left, as we have seen, a large number of negroes helpless and homeless in Britain, and to aid them the African Society was formed under the emancipationists, Wilberforce, Zachary Macaulay and Granville Sharp.

The scheme which they sponsored was an attempt to set up a colony of free negroes in Sierra Leone. Seven hundred ex-slaves volunteered to go as pioneers in this experiment. The first disaster was the publication at the same time of a plan for a convict settlement in New South Wales, to which convicted criminals might be transported for life. The slaves had no reason to trust

or love the British officials, and some three hundred refused to sail for Sierra Leone, believing that the Government was merely trapping them into an even worse form
of slavery, a convict settlement in Africa.

Of those who did go, half died of fever in the un-
accustomed climate, and the homes of the rest were
burned down by a local chief in revenge for a fancied
slight.

In 1791, the year of Wesley's death and Coke's
eclipse, eleven hundred negroes were sent from Nova
Scotia. Many of them had fought beside the British
soldiers in America and, with them, had sought a home
in the British colony of Canada next door. They fell
sick and died in the extreme cold of Nova Scotia, and
eagerly responded to the opportunity of returning to
their homeland. These families were the founders of
Freetown, and included a number of men who had been
converted under Methodist preaching either in America
or in the army.

The colony was augmented by the arrival of freemen
from the West Indies and negroes who were freed from
French or Portuguese slave-trading vessels off the
African coast. Despite an attack by a French squadron
in 1794, the colony maintained its life.

In 1792 there were over two hundred and twenty
Methodists there, and they sent to Coke imploring him
to obtain school-teachers and preachers for them. Coke
leaped at the opportunity, but his enthusiasm must
have impaired his judgment, for the men who went out
as teachers with Governor Macaulay in 1795 refused to
move inland, and the whole venture was a complete
failure.

The next year Coke managed to get the Conference
to agree to two missionaries being appointed, no doubt

following Wilberforce's strong plea for Methodist support in the campaign for the abolition of the slave-trade
with an equally eloquent claim for practical aid to those
who were already free. In spite of this, neither of the
missionaries sailed for Sierra Leone. One went to the
West Indies and the other to Ireland.

It was twelve years before he tried again to move the
Conference. Then, a Methodist class-leader in Sierra
Leone wrote to say that already one chapel had been
built, another was being erected and many of the
maroons were being converted. Coke appealed for
volunteers, and in Helston, two years later, he found
a man of his own mind. George Warren was willing
to go.

In 1811 Warren and three others sailed for West
Africa, the first men to put into practice Coke's long
dream of a mission to Africa and the East. They provided the first martyr-missionary of the Methodist
Church, in Africa or Asia. George Warren died after
eight months, one of the others returned at the same
time broken in health, and the remaining two came home
a few years later. But the mission, once begun, did not
cease its work, though its history has gaps following the
death or breakdown of those who volunteered, year
after year.

This decade saw Coke's dream becoming real in other
fields. In Burslem he met young Samuel Leigh, who
was brought up in the Established Church, became an
Independent and found his home, finally, in Methodism. Coke infected him with his love of people whom
neither had seen, and Leigh began to plan his life in
terms of service overseas. He was willing to go to
America but the appointment was cancelled as the ship
was about to sail, and a couple of years after Coke's

death he became the first British missionary to the South Seas.

A letter which appeared in the *Methodist Magazine,* signed by "J. Kendrick," drew his attention to South Africa. The writer asked that his letter be brought to the notice of Dr. Coke, whose name was known by men and women all over the world, and urged that something be done for the British garrisons in South Africa, who had no chaplains of their own convictions. There was the possibility of work for them, too, amongst the population of the country. The writer died before the answer came, but here, as before, Coke stepped in and persuaded the Conference to appoint a minister for this work. The new recruit, who sailed a short while after Coke himself, was to be followed by others who would dare the great trek northwards across the veldt which was to result in the establishment of Methodist missions throughout the Union.

It should not be forgotten that, though the United States had a growing, virile Methodism of its own, Canada, with the maritime provinces, and Newfoundland, were partly under the control of British Methodism, and its ministry, other than that which was raised up amongst the colonists themselves, had to be supplied from the ranks of the preachers in Britain. It was a hard life, far more rigorous in some ways than that of the missionaries in the West Indies, and it demanded constant understanding and supervision. It had its failures, and they were not surprising, but it had moments of triumph which rejoiced Coke's heart.

To how much does this missionary labour amount in 1812?

There is a growing Church in the West Indies, supported to some extent by its own members, together with gifts from Coke, who had visited the islands half a dozen times at his own expense.

The work in Canada, outcome of British Methodist commitments in the American Colonies, is widespread in the East, and makes demands on the British Conference for men and money.

There are one missionary and three teachers in Sierra Leone, who have been there for less than a year.

There are no missionaries in South Africa, Ceylon, India, the East Indies or the South Seas.

It is not a notable record for a Church which has been listening to the pleading, sometimes the anguished appeals, of Coke for twenty-six years. It is even less glorious when it is realised how much labour, and sometimes humiliation, Coke had gone to in raising the funds for its support. It is only ten years since the Conference has authorised the taking of collections for the support of missionary work. Some of the men who are to be the most distinguished leaders of Methodism in the next generation, are already powerful fellow-advocates—Watson and Bunting amongst them—but the funds of the Missionary Committee are almost hopelessly in debt, despite Coke's immense personal generosity.

How great that generosity is the Church hardly realises.

Before he was married, Coke had an annual income of about twelve hundred pounds. To this was added a considerable fortune when he married Miss Smith, though she kept the control of her own money.

Whenever an appeal was made by Wesley for money for any object, Coke responded. There was an appeal for a new preaching-place in Dewsbury, for instance. Wesley asked the Conference to raise the money—two hundred pounds. It was raised almost at once. Wesley gave fifty pounds. Coke gave fifty pounds. The two hundred members of the Conference gave the remaining hundred.

In the *Plan for Missions,* Coke's own name headed the list of subscribers.

Before the turn of the century he had given a thousand pounds directly to the West Indies, as well as the payment of his passage-money on his tours of supervision. In addition, in 1797, there was a debt for building churches in the West Indies due to him which he forgave—he had advanced twelve hundred pounds and took none of it back.

His wife's large fortune was almost all given to the cause they both loved before she died in 1810.

Yet Methodism still refused to respond in any way to his great missionary appeal for the East.

Coke was only encouraged by the work in the West Indies; he was not satisfied by it. It confirmed his belief that Methodism was born to be a missionary Church. No success in the West and no venture in Africa could make him forget his great longing—to see a mission begun in the East, and to lead it himself.

He yearned for the opportunity of going to India, but something more decisive than the indifference of Methodism had prevented his planning such a scheme. The East India Company, the powerful trading concern which represented British interests in India, and which had established itself by conquest in wars with French, Dutch and local Indian rulers, was adamant in its refusal to allow any kind of missionary work in the areas it controlled. The Company permitted chaplains to minister to its own troops, but refused them permission—which few, in any case, would have desired—to

"interfere" in the religious affairs of the Indian people.
Heavy punishments were set down for any who dared
to break this rule.

Wilberforce had persuaded William Pitt to introduce
a clause in his India Bill of 1783 granting the right of
preaching to the Indian people, but the matter was
defeated after an acrimonious Parliamentary debate,
and did not arise again for thirty years. The financial
interests of the Company were too strong for interference in so small a matter from Britain, even had
there been a much greater concern about the matter
than there was. When William Carey and his friends
undertook the first Protestant mission to Bengal on
behalf of the Baptist Church, he was forced to live and
work, not in the British area, but in the neighbouring
Danish colony of Serampore.

Though it was futile to plan for a mission to India,
Coke could not forget the dream he had cherished
through the years. His correspondence with Sir Charles
Grant, a powerful civil servant who became known, for
his influence amongst the directors of the East India
Company, as the "ruler of the rulers of India," confirmed him in his desires. If India could not be reached
in one way, then he would reach it in another.

His next action was probably the most foolish of all his
wayward and impulsive schemes. No man had been
more vigorous in widening the gap between the Establishment and Methodism, despite his love for his mother
Church. He had preached without leave in whose-ever
parish he wished. He had been active in drawing up the
legal documents which made for the stability of
Methodism as a separate communion and, in 1797, had
presided over the very Conference which accepted the
principle of separation. He had strongly supported

movements for the holding of Methodist services during the hours of worship in the parish churches, against Wesley's will. He had been one of the most conspicuous agents in the raising up of a new Church in America, when the authorities in England had refused to serve the colonists. In order to do so, he had been amongst the first to acknowledge and accept "ordination"—that spiritual arrogation of the episcopacy alone —at the hands of a presbyter. He had even had the presumptuous bad taste to call himself "bishop" in America, and try to make Methodists agree to the creation of yet more "bishops" in their separated society in England. Such was the judgment of the Church of England.

In face of this history of irregularity and indiscipline Coke suggested to the authorities of the Church and State that he be raised to the episcopate and sent to India as the first Anglican bishop in that country.

In fairness to his inward conviction it must be said that he did not even tell the truth in his application. He presented himself as one who wished to serve the European community in India, and minister to the Hindus in his spare time. There is no doubt that, had the fantastic scheme been approved, he would have wished to begin a mission at once to the Indian people and would have left most of the work amongst Europeans to his lower clergy.

There could never have been any doubt about the results of such an action. It made him slightly ridiculous in the eyes of many outside of Methodism, and highly suspect by those within. That he was willing, after prolonged thought and consideration with friends who did their best to dissuade him, so to expose himself to misrepresentation, is a measure of the conviction which now would not be shaken that he must somehow reach India.

When it was quite evident that India must be put out of consideration for the time, he concentrated on trying to gain permission to lead a mission to Ceylon and Java. In both places more tolerance would be found, and in Ceylon, at any rate, there were a few Methodist people who would be only too eager to help.

He pleaded, he cajoled, he wept before his brethren. He raised money and reduced his own resources year after year. Methodism was adamant. The war, the home missions, affairs in Canada and the West Indies, Coke's own age, a score of other reasons were put forward to prove how impossible was a mission to the East.

In the early part of 1813 the long-standing decision of the East India Company refusing permission for missionaries to enter British India was revoked.

In the summer of the same year, at the Liverpool Conference, Coke made his last appeal.

The oldest Methodist Church in Asia, Colombo, Ceylon. Built 1816.
The house to the right is the original Mission House.

CHAPTER TEN

THE GREAT APPEAL
(1813)

DR. COKE, no longer the raven-haired, sprightly, flushed young man who had won so many hearts in Ireland and America, but showing more signs of his age than many men of his sixty-six years, sat at a table in Dublin. He read over once more the letter he had received. It reminded him that he had crossed the Atlantic eighteen times, that he was an old man, that he would find it difficult now to learn a foreign language, that there was no one to take his place in Methodism as the great inspirer and supporter of missionary work. He laid it down and took up his pen.

He set down the date—June 28th, 1813. And the place—the preaching-house, Dublin.

Then, without pausing long to think, for his heart was full, he began to write.

"I beg pardon for being so long in answering your letter. I have laboured in the begging way since the last Conference more arduously than ever. . . . I am now dead to Europe, and alive to India. God Himself has said to me: 'Go to Ceylon.' I am so fully convinced of the will of God that methinks I had rather be set naked on the coast of Ceylon, without clothes, and without a friend, than not go there. . . ."

A day or two later he returned to England, to attend the English Conference at Liverpool.

There had already, in May, been a meeting of

preachers in London, which had discussed at some length Coke's renewed plan for a mission to Ceylon and India, and had decided against it. Several of the more senior London preachers made it quite clear when they arrived in Liverpool that they had not changed their minds.

Coke, nevertheless, had continued both to raise money and to canvass recruits amongst the preachers during the year, and he came to the Conference knowing that a dozen or more men, some of them with their wives, were ready to go with him if the Conference would agree.

Such agreement seemed remote. Discussion had brought some of the greatest of the preachers to his side, and one of his friends had preached the official sermon to the Conference with definite reference to the decision they were to make. The debate continued throughout the day, and when the business was adjourned, unfinished, it seemed clear that the next morning would see the project once more defeated.

Coke wept openly in the street as he went to his lodging.

The next morning he did not come to the early session of the Conference, and the debate was left until his arrival. Some of his friends, anxious in case the previous day had been too much for his obviously failing health, went to look for him. They found him uneasy, pacing his room. It was clear that he had not slept throughout the night, and he told them that he had spent the dark hours on his knees, praying for India. Gathering his papers together, he left his lodging with them and went to the Conference chapel.

The President called on him to speak, and he replied clearly, simply, in the voice that had moved so many all over the western world. It was not a strong voice, and occasionally they had to listen closely to catch what he said.

He recounted the providential way in which missionary work had first begun in the West Indies. He went on to point out that a new sympathy was being shown by those in authority to plans for the East. He insisted on the responsibility of those who knew the gospel for preaching to those who had never heard it. He drew to an end, and offered once more to the Conference, his own services and those who, with him, were willing to dare the dangers of the new enterprise.

His friends were deeply moved, his critics touched, but unconvinced. The design was too great to be practicable.

He paused for a moment, and then made his last appeal.

"If the connexion cannot furnish the expense, I will be prepared to devote the rest of my fortune to defray the expenses necessary for the outfitting and commencement of this work, to the extent of six thousand pounds."

He sat down in silence.

Before the end of the day, the Conference, awed and humbled by a man who gave himself and all he had to the cause he had pleaded with such devotion, authorised and appointed him to undertake a mission to Ceylon and Java, and allowed him to take six missionaries with him, exclusive of one for the Cape of Good Hope.

In the weeks that followed Coke was never at rest. He busied himself with gaining letters of recommendation which would help the missionaries when they landed. He arranged for tutors in Dutch and Portuguese, the languages of Ceylon other than Tamil and Sinhalese, for which no teachers could be found, and made certain that his colleagues had begun to study hard before they left England. He himself had already become reasonably proficient in Portuguese before the meeting of Conference. He made arrangements to secure passages, and began at once to collect the equipment necessary to the expedition.

In his methods of setting up the missionaries with clothes, books and other effects he was prodigal in the extreme, at any rate in the opinion of the Missionary Committee, whom he never consulted in any way about his purchases. They were highly critical of some of them. Coke, with characteristic and impulsive generosity, told them to make a list of what they regarded as essential and he himself would pay for the remainder. In addition, he paid for the customs duties and poundage on the things they were exporting.

One piece of equipment which the Committee questioned but which made a great deal of difference to the effectiveness of the work in Ceylon was a printing-press, which he purchased for two hundred pounds. Fortunately, two of the missionaries had been apprenticed as printers in their early days.

Towards the end of the year, passages were secured in two sailing-vessels, belonging to the famous fleet of East Indiamen—the *Cabalva* and the *Lady Melville*. The party, to save undue expense, had to split up, Clough and Harvard sailing with Coke in the *Cabalva*, and Ault, Lynch, Erskine and Squance in the other ship. When the passages had been booked the designated missionaries were ordained and, on December 10th, news having been received that the vessels had left the Thames to join the East Indies fleet at Portsmouth, the party set out, following their own ways, and met at the Bush Hotel there.

When they arrived Coke rose from his chair and prayed with them. He was deeply moved as they came to the last town they were to lodge in in England. "Here we all are before God," he exclaimed, "now embarked in the most glorious and the most important work in the world." For nearly three weeks they remained in Portsmouth, and the missionaries preached on the two intervening Sundays to crowded, fascinated congregations.

Coke's last text was: "Ethiopia shall soon stretch out her hands to God." Towards the end of his sermon he said, in summary of his life-long conviction, "I am fully persuaded that we who are about to leave you, are in the path of duty; and I am perfectly convinced that God will bless our labours, though to what extent and in what manner may be unknown. . . . Let me beseech you not to estimate the probability of our success by the insignificance of the instruments: the work is of God. There was a time when Christianity itself had, in all human probability, less to hope. The powers which favour us were hostile to it; and yet, in three hundred years it rose upon the ruins of Paganism. Who can say that a similar result may not take place among the millions of India, whose future generations shall rise up and call us blessed?"

On December 30th the commodore's guns sounded and the fleet began to loosen its moorings. A note came from Captain Birch to tell Coke and his companions that the *Cabalva* was under way and he was wanted on board. He passed through the crowds of sailors and visitors, coming to see the fleet set sail, as he made his way to the docks. He hardly noticed them, any more than he saw the inns made famous by kings and admirals who had rested in them after long years of defeat or victory on sea and land. He, too, was setting out on a campaign, more important perhaps, he knew, than the last on which Nelson had set out ten years before. That saved Britain; this might, by the grace of God, save the Eastern world.

He took his place in the small boat which was waiting to row him to the great vessel offshore, her decks full of scurrying figures and some of her sails already set. He sat in the stern with folded hands, and saw no one. He did not wave. He never even said farewell. A little while later he scaled the rope-ladder and stood on deck. For a moment his eyes wandered across the water to the English land beyond. Then he went down, with Harvard and Clough, to their cabins.

The next morning, the last day of the year 1813, the sails were hoisted and the convoy moved out into the Channel.

CHAPTER ELEVEN

THE END
(1814)

THE voyage was to be longer than any Coke had undertaken previously, and he was prepared to make the best use of it. He began to work at his language study as soon as they were off the Isle of Wight, and continued to do so until they reached the Indian Ocean. In addition, he had his own *Commentary* and a store of books. Fortunately, he was a good sailor, and the mountainous seas left him less disturbed than they did some of his colleagues, for, from the beginning, the voyage was to be a perilous one.

They had been at sea a week when they ran into a gale in the Bay of Biscay. Distress signals were seen from one of the ships in the convoy, but by morning she had disappeared and was never heard of again. A fortnight later, off Gibraltar, six more foundered, and the frigate which was sent to assist them never rejoined the convoy.

It had been intended to make a landfall at Madeira, but the gales were still so great that they decided to avoid risking the ships and continue south to the Cape. A homeward-bound fleet of forty ships passed them close at hand, and the Captain signalled to them by trumpets as they sailed close by. Signal communication was maintained with their own fleet, and brought them the sad news that Mrs. Ault, about whose health grave doubts had been felt before they left England, was seriously ill, and when a period of calm allowed some passage between the two ships, Harvard and Clough took the opportunity of visiting the *Lady Melville*. They brought back the sad news that Mrs. Ault had died and been buried at sea.

As they neared the Cape of Good Hope fresh gales blew up, and disasters began to overtake the sailors who tried to attend to the sails and rigging. Several fell on the deck and were killed, or fell into the sea and were drowned. A number of soldiers, unused to the sea and in poor accommodation, were overcome by the conditions they had to live in and died before they saw land.

At the Cape most of the fleet stood well out, but the *Cabalva* touched land long enough for letters to be handed ashore for despatch to England.

One of the deprivations of the voyage was that, in spite of having three ministers on board, no services were permitted, as the East India Company, in its passionate disregard for religion, refused to allow public worship in its ships to be conducted by anyone other than the Captain. Captain Birch, though resenting the regulation, could not disobey his orders, though he encouraged Coke to read his *Commentary* aloud to the passengers and to pray with them and visit the soldiers in place of a chaplain.

The voyage went on, now and then in tempestuous gales, and continually in appalling heat. Sailors and passengers alike sickened. Harvard was taken ill, and so was his wife. Good Friday and Easter Day passed by, and they sailed slowly under the burning sun of the Indian Ocean. Coke saw India drawing nearer day by day, and planned and prayed for the hour to come when he would first see the people he had served so lovingly throughout his life. April came, and went, and the doctor spent more and more time at his books and his translating of the Scriptures.

"Food and medicine, shield and sword,
Jesus gives me in His word"

he wrote in his *Journal*. So greatly did he tax himself that his friends grew anxious and urged him to take more rest. Whenever a ship was sighted, or a shoal of dolphins, or a shark was caught, Clough would call him up to see what was happening. But nothing could keep him on deck. Back he went to his preparations and his plans.

At the beginning of May he looked more weary than his friends had ever seen him. He was more withdrawn and relaxed, and seemed to see nothing around him. He was already living in Ceylon. The next night he went to lie down early, taking a glass of medicine with him to relieve the pain he felt.

The servant went to his cabin at half-past five the next morning, May 3rd, and knocked. There was no answer. He knocked again, and opened the door.

Thomas Coke lay on the floor, where he had fallen at his prayers. When they went to him he was quite dead. The doctor told them he must have been dead some time. He had died of apoplexy.

At five o'clock that afternoon they buried his body at sea, not far from the island of Galega, in the Indian Ocean.

Eighteen days later the guns of the fort in Bombay were fired in salute as the East Indiamen came into harbour. About a month afterwards the missionaries landed at Galle, in Ceylon, and looked about them at the land which, for almost thirty years, Doctor Coke had longed to see.

The mission to the East had begun.

THE WORLD HE WON

THE man who wanted the world for Christ was dead.

Until the very end of his life he had been circumscribed and frustrated, even by some of the greatest leaders in Methodism, and, though many of the Methodist people, after the turn of the century, had been convinced of the rightness of the cause he pleaded, the responsible courts of the Church had withstood his passionate appeals until his final act of self-sacrifice had made further opposition impossible. It is true that he had seen a great work going forward in America, where he was highly honoured, and had witnessed the birth of a noble Church in the West Indies, but he had been deprived of doing the very thing he so fervently desired: the carrying of the gospel to the East. He never set foot in Africa, though he had seen its coastline, and he never even looked on Ceylon or India, the lands of his dreams.

What had he achieved?

When he died, it seemed little enough. Five years, even two years, later it was evident that he had set Methodism on fire again, as, in the century that had gone, John Wesley had kindled England to a blaze. His death at sea on the eve of his new mission shook the whole of Methodism, and did much to confirm the people in their new sense of purpose and dedication.

From the moment when he stood up in Liverpool and offered himself and his fortune the missionary impulse quickened, and soon the Methodist Church was throbbing with new life. Before he left England, in October a meeting was held in Leeds which inaugurated the Methodist Missionary Society. Two years later the first public meeting of the Missionary Society was held in Manchester, and three years afterwards the Society took over its first offices in City Road.

It is not by meetings, or offices, or societies, however, that we judge his greatness or success. It is by what suddenly began to happen overseas. Not even his bright hopefulness could have foreseen the tremendous vigour with which the work went forward in East and West.

Some developments could have been expected, others were surprising in their virility. For instance, there was already a strong Church in the West Indies, which spread from island to island as the years passed. Persecution of the slave-members and the missionaries grew more intense as emancipation drew nearer, but this served only to strengthen the life and witness of Methodism. In Canada, where the work had been long established in the maritime provinces, new pioneering adventures took the preachers into the prairies and the backwoods, and resulted not only in the evangelising of the colonists but the conversion of the Red Indians. The American Methodist Church was already wielding tremendous influence in national and social affairs throughout the United States.

It was in the lands where no missionaries had yet worked that the Church found its great opportunities and challenges. North Ceylon was opened up, and preaching, teaching and the printed word made a passage for the Gospel. Within four or five years of the arrival of Coke's colleagues, the New Testament had been translated and printed in Portuguese, and the whole Bible in Sinhalese. Lynch, who sailed with Coke, led the way across from Ceylon into India, where he found little groups of soldiers already at work amongst the people, and bases were quickly established in Madras, Bangalore, and Trichinopoly area and Bombay.

George Warren, the first missionary to Sierra Leone, died after being only a few months on the Coast, but this did not prevent a stream of men and women following him into a district which became known as the "white man's grave." Some of those who went died after only a week or two on the Coast, others lasted for months, some for a few years before death or ill-health claimed them. Nothing could stop the volunteers for the West Coast. Its very dangers drew some of the bravest spirits, and the West African Church is built on their heroic self-sacrifice.

The year after Coke's death, Samuel Leigh arrived in Australia and later in New Zealand, the first Methodist preacher in the South Seas. In spite of the colonists' primary concern with copper and gold mining in Australia, and the attacks of the Maoris in New Zealand, the work went forward rapidly, and it was not long before the lure of preaching to the cannibal islanders of Samoa, Fiji and Tonga drew more adventurous spirits into these lovely but dangerous places.

Sergeant Kendrick's letter about South Africa was soon answered. The first preacher to land in South Africa, a few months after Coke set out for the East, found his work hindered by the military authorities, but the two great pioneers who followed him—Barnabas and William Shaw—trekked northwards across the veldt to the lands of the Kaffirs and the Zulus, and very soon, under great hardships, the missionaries were at work in the interior.

Coke's hopes of Protestant missions in France were not long in being realised, and Methodism began a sturdy witness not only there, but in the Scandinavian countries and Germany, and in the Catholic countries along the Mediterranean Sea. Work was begun, though it was later abandoned, in Egypt and Palestine, amongst the Arabs.

Two years after Coke's death there were one hundred and eleven missionaries overseas, in Europe, the West Indies, Canada, South and West Africa, Ceylon and India, Australia, New Zealand and the South Seas. The membership of the overseas Church had grown to twenty-three thousand.

Still greater things lay ahead. In 1840 the first negro candidate for the ministry came to Britain to be trained at Richmond College. Towards the middle of the century, Australia, South Africa and Canada had all progressed so rapidly that they were able to maintain their own Methodist Conferences, governing their own colonial Methodist Church and, what is more significant, ordering their own missionary work. Places Coke left out of his plans were evangelised—Burma and China amongst them.

Not until the whole missionary story can be written can the importance of Thomas Coke be fully assessed. He belongs to the whole world, which he loved and lived for. In spite of all his defects, he remains a towering, dynamic figure amongst the leaders of the Church. He was, without doubt, the father, not only of Methodist missions, but of all modern Protestant missions. He was a preacher with a passion for evangelism, an organiser who commanded men by his zealous spirit rather than his position of authority, an administrator with a world-wide vision. If he was impetuous, it was because he could not believe that any obstacle could stand in the way of the Kingdom of God; if he was ambitious, he was ambitious for Christ's glory and not his own. Tireless, indomitable, readily daring a life of peril when he might have sat at ease, living in insecurity and dying at his task, he roused a lethargic Methodism, much preoccupied with its own local affairs, not only to a sense of responsibility for the world, but to a passionate devotion to the Christ whom he served, and to a new love for the men and women of every race and colour for whom Christ died.

He did not die in vain.

Nor will his story have been remembered in vain if it kindles in the Church, and especially the youth of the Church, something of that flame which consumed him and set fire to the nations in his own day.

INDEX